The Uncertain
Business of Doing Good

THE UNCERTAIN
BUSINESS OF DOING GOOD

OUTSIDERS IN AFRICA

LARRY KROTZ

UNIVERSITY OF MANITOBA PRESS

University of Manitoba Press
Winnipeg, Manitoba R3T 2N2 Canada
www.umanitoba.ca/uofmpress

Printed in Canada by Friesens.

Cover design: Doowah Design
Text design: Relish Design Studio
Maps: Weldon Hiebert
Cover photo: Larry Krotz

Library and Archives Canada Cataloguing in Publication

Krotz, Larry, 1948-
     The uncertain business of doing good : outsiders in Africa / Larry Krotz.

Includes bibliographical references.
ISBN 978-0-88755-707-1 (pbk.)

     1. Economic assistance--Africa. 2. Africa--Economic conditions--1960-.
3. Africa--Social conditions--1960-. 4. Africa--Politics and government--1960-.
5. Poverty--Africa. I. Title.

HC800.K76 2008   338.91096   C2008-902231-9

The University of Manitoba gratefully acknowledges the financial support for its
publication program provided by the Government of Canada through the Book
Publishing Industry Development Program (BPIDP), the Canada Council for the
Arts, the Manitoba Arts Council, and the Manitoba Department of Culture,
Heritage, and Tourism.

Mixed Sources
www.fsc.org Cert no. SW-COC-1271
© 1996 Forest Stewardship Council
FSC

All the news out of Africa is bad. It made me want to go there.
— Paul Theroux, *Dark Star Safari*

CONTENTS

ACKNOWLEDGEMENTS

*A*T VARIOUS STAGES OF RESEARCH AND WRITING, I received financial support for this book from the Manitoba Arts Council and the Ontario Arts Council. I want to acknowledge, with gratitude, their assistance.

My initial documentary filmmaking and journalistic forays into Africa were made at the behest of the National Film Board of Canada, Vision Television, and publications: the *National Post*, *Saturday Night* magazine, the *United Church Observer*, the *Walrus* magazine. I want to thank them for their encouragement and support, as I likewise want to thank some individuals who were encouraging and helpful to me. Hugh McCullum was my host on two occasions in Harare and remains a steady friend and sounding board re Africa and ideas. Jim Kirkwood of the United Church and Africafiles encouraged me in my first trip to Angola.

In order to keep my ideas on track throughout the writing, I depended heavily on friends Paul Wilson and Patricia Grant, and on my wife, Stephanie Leontowitsch, for perceptive insights and criticisms. Then, when it finally came to publishing, I have been delighted to work with the University of Manitoba Press. The support and faith shown by David Carr, the sure editing eye of Pat Sanders, and the assistance of Cheryl Miki have been invaluable.

Finally, there would be no book without the generous access granted by all the people you will find in the book, the medical scientists, the genocide trial lawyers, the foreign aid workers, and the local people of the various communities and projects who show up in the pages and chapters. Of these I want to make special mention of Ian Maclean, who has been a steady and reliable help in understanding the complexities of AIDS research and science and a good friend and guide, especially around Nairobi and Kisumu in Kenya with an understanding of absolutely the best curry and local fare restaurants.

THE UNCERTAIN
BUSINESS OF DOING GOOD

DETAIL OF AFRICA

Introduction

OUTSIDERS IN AFRICA

*W*HEN YOU PICK UP A BOOK ABOUT AFRICA, it is almost inevitably not so much about Africa as about us. Africa is an obsession for a great many people, even some who have never set foot there. Though a continent of fifty-some countries and almost three quarters of a billion people, it is, especially for the Westerner, the European, or the North American, very much a place of the mind and the imagination. The very word, "Africa," has the power to elicit longing and fantasy. In turn, it carries a great and perhaps unfair burden: that of fulfilling some of our deepest needs. Africa reassures us about what might still be left of a wild world with deep jungles, massive pachyderms, and dangerous felines; it provides a home for the fossilized bones of our ancient ancestors; it offers an object for our altruistic impulses. It is the kind of place that if it didn't already exist, we might well have to invent.

Africa is sufficiently exotic, and far enough away, that outsiders have always been able to approach it with a kind of untroubled certainty. This was true whether there was blatant exploitation on their minds or more benign purposes. It is no less the case for someone looking to cure HIV/

AIDS or prod development in the early years of the twenty-first century than it was when the motivating forces were anti-slavery, missionizing for Christianity, or delivering the 'benefits' of colonialism in the nineteenth and twentieth centuries. Part and parcel of the package is an assumption of ownership, possession that one takes either literally, as did the nineteenth-century colonialists, or in a more figurative, emotional, or psychological sense. On television I have just seen Margaret Trudeau, the former wife of the late prime minister, freshly returned from an Ethiopian village where a charity she participates in has installed water tanks. She told the interviewer, with not the slightest irony, about "my Africa." At the same time, the pop star, Madonna, has just come back with great fanfare and some controversy from picking up a newly adopted child from an orphanage in Malawi. Though this was reportedly her first trip to the continent, let alone the country, she had promised to give millions to such orphans, so why shouldn't she be allowed to take one of them home? We presume a great deal when it comes to Africa, often letting that presumption spill out without the least sense of shame or even self-consciousness.

In 1992 I made my first visit to Africa. My story is simple. I have always worked as a writer and a filmmaker, and had been offered the opportunity of a lifetime, to make a documentary film in Angola. It is astonishing how easily such things come about. The action of hopping on a plane and being transported in short order to someplace far away, even someplace improbable, has become commonplace. It has a great deal to do, of course, with who you are. You don't have to be rich, just well-placed and sort of lucky—being North American or European helps—and then you can go absolutely anywhere, taking it calmly for granted you will be returned intact, a matter I find not insubstantial as a definer of the age in which we live. In my case I had been writing journalism for magazines and making programs for an educational television service. Somebody had seen my work, one thing led to another, and there I was. There were going to be three of us on our little team, the assignment to look at a country struggling through turmoil and then produce articles and a news-style documentary that might attempt to explain things. Upon reflection, we realized we were going to be foreign correspondents, something, I confess, that fulfilled a long-held romantic fantasy. There are numerous ways to move about the world, as a tourist, on business, as an explorer, a diplomat, a soldier, a missionary or some equivalent do-gooder, an immigrant or refugee. None of these has quite the cachet of "foreign correspondent." I also have to admit I didn't properly know where Angola was and had to look it up on a map. It was below the equator, which meant water going down the drains spun counter-clockwise.

On the way to Angola I went to Zimbabwe, where I had friends who'd invited me to visit and from where our film enterprise would be organized with a local crew and equipment. After what seemed an endless overnight flight from London, the plane touched down in the capital city, Harare. Zimbabwe is an exceedingly beautiful country, which at that time hadn't yet fallen apart into the complete mess it has become fifteen years later. AIDS wasn't as bad as it would become, nor were food shortages or the public corruption and cruelty of the president. The banks, newspapers, and transportation systems still worked. I did what business I needed to do and then, with time on my hands, took off to have a look at one of the natural wonders of the country—indeed, the world—Victoria Falls.

It was an hour's trip in a small twenty-seater airplane. From the window I looked down on farms and bush and then, abruptly, spotted what looked like a great cloud on the horizon. "That," my seatmate told me, "is Victoria Falls." It was not the actual falls but the huge plume of mist and evaporating spray that wafts hundreds of metres into the air and then hovers, a dense and unmoving cloud above where the seven individual cataracts of the Zambezi tumble over their 108-metre drop. This vapour landmark has earned the place, since as long ago as the first human with language came upon it, the moniker *Mosi-oa-tunya* ("smoke that thunders"). On the ground I got myself settled, then set out to explore. To see the falls, you followed well-trodden paths through the bush. I made it to the lip of the most accessible of the cataracts, and then walked along a rickety fence made out of thorn sticks until I reached another tumble of the river, and then another. Spray soaked me to the skin but, just as quickly, the hot sun dried me off. Pushing forward, I reached a clearing where, totally unexpectedly, I bumped up against something that stood out starkly against the underbrush: a statue, erect and forward-looking, cast in bronze and painted green. Doctor David Livingstone, the first white person to see the falls, and therefore to "discover it" and claim it in all its wonder in the name of the British Queen.

The moment moved me greatly; every Westerner knows about Livingstone, but for me, encountering the statue had additional impact, not least because one of my grandmothers, one who died before I was born, had worked when a girl as household help for a family of Livingstones in our town in Canada. They were a couple of times removed but descendants nonetheless and their affiliation, plus my grandmother's connection, caused our own family to believe we too almost owned the great missionary doctor and all his righteous deeds. In the sixth grade I wrote a history essay that claimed him as a sort of talismanic hero and now here I was on a spot where he had once stood, though many kilometres from the place much further north where his intrepid heart lay buried. I walked back to the colonial-style hotel where all the rich tourists outfitted by Abercrombie and Fitch, or at least Ralph Lauren, to look like latter-day Henry Morton Stanleys like to stay. I slipped in among them and ordered from the immaculate waiter my own gin with tonic. Then I went back to Harare and off to Angola.

Over the next decade and a half, I got lucky, making numerous return trips to a number of African countries. My role was always specific: journalist, writer, documentary maker. Much of the time I travelled in the company of other outsiders, North Americans or Europeans, in order to report on them because they were involved in 'projects'. These were not celebrities, like Margaret Trudeau or Madonna, but serious on-the-ground people, foreign aid workers, peacekeepers, medical scientists, lawyers, and jurists. They were, to a person, hard workers with ambitious missions, like trying to broker peace and reconstruction at the end of Angola's civil war and help run that country's first elections, find ways to combat HIV/AIDS and even search for a cure, or bring justice in the aftermath of Rwanda. For my part I considered myself the most fortunate of travellers, assigned to report about some of the most pressing problems of our day—refugees,

AIDS, genocides—and on one level the stories were enough, I could record adventures loaded with their own internal drama. But as things progressed, I noted that something grew to be more important: inside each enterprise was implied a relationship—not only implied but necessitated—between the outsiders and the place and people we were visiting. And this is what I started paying attention to. Whether aid workers and peacekeepers in Angola, AIDS scientists and medical researchers conducting clinical trials in Kenya, lawyers and jurists at the United Nations tribunal for Rwanda in Tanzania, we foreigners, including, of course, me, the travelling writer, were entering and affecting other people's worlds. In so doing, our smallest action, including where we chose to stay, what we chose to eat, how we behaved ourselves, certainly whom among the locals we selected to work for or with us, held meaning. The big question was, though, who were we? And even more, who did those we were visiting think we were?

At bottom, every enterprise recounted in this book has to do with one of the most complex undertakings in human activity: the project of 'doing good'. None of the people I spent my time with would characterize themselves overtly as do-gooders. They would be, in fact, deeply (and properly) skeptical of the term, far more likely to define themselves by their skills as soldiers/ peacekeepers, elections and political science specialists, jurists, microbiologists, and researchers. Their work, for the most part, was not even connected to such things as overt poverty-ending projects. Indeed, with the exception of only a couple, these people were positioned some distance from 'development work'. Yet, as members of the cadres of foreigners with the kind of expertise that was taken for granted to surpass local African expertise, they had landed into the tricky territory of giving if not imposing a kind of 'good'. Doing good was the (usually unspoken but always present) justification, the argument, the excuse, and from time to time perhaps also the curse. The biggest items we all carried in our luggage were exalted motives.

"Doing good" is one of those terms that is hard to define in a tidy, all-encompassing way. It can be the action of responding to requests for aid from those in need, but it can also be an action of presumption: defining needs independent of the wishes of a targeted people and inserting/asserting oneself into that situation. Both undertakings are tricky. In the former, a relationship of care and trust is demanded with strict limits; people asking for help have already put their dignity on the line. The latter, however, is even more chancy, for it not only intrudes on the lives of a designated people but can lead to—or stem from—delusions on the part of the deliverers. The most gross example of this is perhaps the notion in the minds of the leadership of the United States and Britain that they were somehow doing good by their invasion of Iraq (or Canada, for that matter, by participating in the "mission" in Afghanistan).

We find it hard, nevertheless, to turn away from either the need or the opportunity to do good, for it cries out at the universal human spirit and is deeply embedded in the culture, certainly, of the West. The American founding father, Thomas Jefferson, wrote, "Nature hath implanted in our breasts a love of others, a sense of duty to them, a moral instinct ... which prompts us irresistibly to feel and succour their distresses."[1] Some not-so-latent missionary spirit persists on a central plinth in our culture, at the core, for example, of much of the narrative of our media that brings us tales of misery and woe, and demands, by implication, action. It is also at the core of what we like to think is the best of our spirit: our idealism, our values of unselfishness, our willingness to share at least the surpluses of our material wealth, our knowledge, our skill and humanity, in a world where those exist in perpetual imbalance. It is hard to decry these moral instincts that at face value should contribute to a better world.

But I carry the story back to Africa, for the peoples of the various countries of that continent over the last couple of centuries have, of all the peoples of the world, been the most targeted by such initiatives. And when we outsiders from the West go off to a place like Africa, what is it precisely that has influenced us? How has our way of thinking about and looking at Africa come to be what it is? To properly think about this, I return to Zimbabwe and revisit that encounter at Victoria Falls with the statue of Doctor Livingstone. The monument, isolated, off in the bush—even a bit forlorn—might easily be dismissed as an icon to a time long past and forgotten. Even my school essay had been in the long-ago and impressionable sixth grade. Yet, arguably, it is a symbol of attitudes that remain fluidly current. What every outsider travelling in Africa needs is an argument and a framework, and for almost two centuries such a framework has been provided by the Scottish missionary. Livingstone created the template, if you will, that has guided in principle as well as a great deal of practice the kind of attitude generations of North Americans and Europeans have come to consider the best sort of attitude to hold toward Africa.

He was, even in his lifetime, a figure of potent myth, one that ballooned to extraordinary proportions when he was feared lost and the search led by the newspaperman sent from America, Henry Morton Stanley, ended with the famous encounter at the grass-hut village of Ujiji on the east shore of Lake Tanganyika and the salutation "Doctor Livingstone, I presume." It then exploded again, shortly after, with Livingstone's death and the sending home of his body wrapped in bark and sealed with pitch to be laid finally into the floor of Westminster Abbey even as his heart remained in Africa, interred beneath the great tree in Chief Chitambo's village. The mythology that grew around the personage of the great doctor, however, is infinitely more simplistic than the actualities of his real life. When examined by serious biographers such as Tim Jeal, his motivations turn out to be complex indeed. Livingstone has been described as a man who became a missionary in order to be a doctor—unlike Schweitzer, almost a century later, who it is said became a doctor in order to become a missionary—and the lad from the impoverished family got his medical education paid for by the Church Mission Society. But the sweep of his influence was far greater than that of a solitary physician. As Jeal wrote: "His ideas, both original and inherited, were to change the way Europeans viewed Africans and Africa itself."[2] Hidden beneath the straightforwardness of his up-front purpose, which was to do good, to heal, to bring medicine, was a more complicated intention. The time when he became interested in Africa, circa 1840, coincided with the apex of the great movements in Britain and America against the slave trade. The predominant organization of the day, whose meetings the young medical student had attended, was called The Society for the Extinction of the Slave Trade and for the Civilization of Africa. It would seem that, slavery already having been outlawed by Britain, the latter purpose was what most caught his fancy. Following from that, the missionary doctor's more complicated motive was decidedly meddlesome. Jeal puts it that what he wanted to do was "undermine tribal institutions by introducing western economics and his ardent propagation of a new form of colonization would have played a crucial part in precipitating the British Government into annexing vast areas of a previously ignored continent."[3]

There were more obviously calculating imperialists. It is, however, easy to dismiss Leopold of the Belgians with his rubber plantations along the River Congo and Rhodes with his search for diamonds in South Africa, history, in fact, already having done that for us. But that Doctor Livingstone too would turn out to be loaded with complicated agendas, more going on than his mythology tells us, is unsettling. Yet it is not right that we be surprised; postcolonial critic Mary Louise Pratt in *Imperial Eyes, Travel Writing and Transculturation* posits that Western medicine has always been "one of the most effective tools of Euro-expansionism."[4] Livingstone was the very vanguard of this. Since first contact, mixtures of messages and mixtures of intentions have been central to the interactions between outsiders and Africa and remain now part of every handshake or conversation or potential partnership, no matter how innocent its surface. That many Africans today cast a skeptical eye on the fleets of white four-wheel-drive Land Rovers racing around their countries is as it should be. They might wish their forebears had been more skeptical of those Land Rovers' pith helmet-wearing antecedents a century ago. For those on the receiving end, the message delivered by visitors who profess to do good can easily appear ambiguous; for those delivering, it is important to know that. What, we might ask, are the tacit agreements or assumptions that govern the relations we outsiders have with local peoples? Is our belief that we bring something useful along with us a pure one, or is it a troubling one— i.e., hegemonic to some degree?

This book is not a polemic, though the continent of Africa with its many problems invites those; you can write about how awful things are, how desperate the poverty, how corrupt the despots who hold power, how violent and destructive the wars and civil strife. You can write about how the actions of foreigners, past and present, have created so many horrible problems. You can write about the enterprises to try to bring improvement:

foreign aid is always ripe for criticism, either because it is seen as too paltry or, on the other side, because no matter how much is spent, it is too often ineffectual, even perpetuating systems and problems. Analyses of this sort have been rolling out in abundance from authorities like William Easterly, a former World Bank economist and professor at New York University, whose *The White Man's Burden: Why the West's Efforts to Aid the Rest Have Done So Much Ill and So Little Good*, published in 2006,[5] charges how, despite half a trillion dollars of foreign aid to Africa over the past forty years, poverty in many countries there has only worsened. Robert Calderisi, another one-time World Bank economist, followed this with his book, *The Trouble with Africa; Why Foreign Aid Isn't Working*,[6] in which he lays the blame at the feet of corrupt local leadership and a global economy that has left Africa behind.

This, however, will be a more personal examination; I am part of each of the stories and harbour the intention not so much to make an argument as look at the intricacies of encounters. I want to examine not so much people's projects or efforts as the attitudes and motivations within which these were initiated, including to reflect on my own attitudes in my role as a writer/journalist/filmmaker transmitting the reports and interpretations back to North America. Recently I had a conversation with a Canadian former missionary who had lived many years in Zambia and who was instrumental in arranging my first trip to Angola. Jim Kirkwood is not a sentimentalist but a critical thinker, firm about the dignity of all peoples and the demands of human justice. What we talked about, though, was a kind of disjunction that I find has a parallel with another type of community where I've spent a great deal of time over the years: Canadian First Nations reserves. When you remove yourself and apply analytical tools, the analysis of either many African situations or many First Nations situations is dispiriting, even devastating. Yet, while you are in them as a visitor, Kirkwood and I agreed, you always have a good time. Through this book I will attempt to get at that perplexing disjunction.

As the title suggests, I have come to believe that of all human activities, seeking to do good sits among our more chancy enterprises. What one needs to confront on the journey through that mine-planted field is innocence as well as power. The power is the power to drop in—almost anywhere we choose—because of our money, our skills, or our connections, as was the case for me when I happened into Angola. The innocence—for I put it to that more than to malevolence or greed or manipulation—is what either disappoints us or causes us to do mischief (often unwitting, always dangerous). The premise I want to explore is how nothing ever turns out to be as simple, straightforward, or as easy as it might seem it should be when one first sets out on it. And following from that, I want to look at what happens when the individual outsider, full of good intentions, lands in some African situation, only to encounter not the certainties he or she might have expected, but nuance, ambiguity, perplexity. I am interested in what happens when the altruistic motive touches the ground, as we intervene to facilitate change for others. I am interested in the confluence of intentions with realities, and in learning whether, when the two do meet, some feedback mechanism, if you like, kicks in to readjust our intentions. Or are we left stymied? Most of all I am interested in the relationships that are both necessary for anything to happen and that develop whilst something is taking place, for they, it seems, are really the only lasting results of any endeavour.

ANGOLA
1992

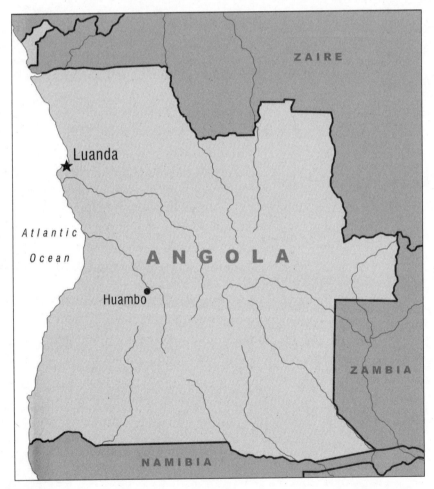

ANGOLA

1

LUANDA

*W*E ARRIVED IN LUANDA, the capital city, in the early evening. The sky was already black as pitch. As the plane came down I could sense more than actually see pinpricks of yellow light struggling up through the misty wash that overlay what I knew must be the city. I'd read somewhere that from outer space, astronauts observed what little light came from the continent of Africa as orange as opposed to the cascades of bright white that paints California, the eastern seaboard of North America, or Europe. Once on the ground, everything was an unremitting black, the kind that can unsettle you, like wakening in the middle of the night in a strange room. The plane, a Portuguese airlines TAP flight, was continuing on to Lisbon and the passengers heading for Europe left their seatbelts fastened. Though a ceasefire had been officially signed in the civil war that had been going on almost without stopping for at least seventeen years since the Portuguese had hightailed it out of their former colony, they weren't taking any chances.[1] Peace of any sort, nonetheless, offered opportunity—which was why we were there—and explained the gambler swagger of many of those disembarking with us. The people staying on board watched us warily, considering us, I suspect, not so much brave adventurers as reckless fools.

When I stepped off the plane, the African night hit me full in the face. There are few sensual pleasures quite like the blast of humid air laced through with suggestions of exotic floral fragrances. I inhaled deeply. The pleasure, though, was short-lived. Inside the terminal building the fragrances were replaced by something else: a hard, dry stench. The building, which we entered after a short walk across the tarmac, was a barn of a place with none of the accoutrements one expects in air terminals. It was a big, echoing hall and, amid a dense din of noise, a sort of anarchy reigned. Ropes had been strung to keep incoming passengers separate from everybody else but they had collapsed and lay, mostly useless, along the concrete floor. As well, it was hard to see; squalls of dim light shed by naked bulbs strung from the rafters were the extent of the illumination. The place was jam-packed, not just with arriving passengers but everybody who was there to meet them, including, I hoped, the contact from the aid agency my employers back in Canada had assured me was going to meet us. And then there was another throng, even larger: the flotilla of hangers-on who, in a country in chaos, seem to find the airport a place of maximum excitement and opportunity, a nerve centre within a culture reduced to day-to-day mode.

I spotted Funcho and Charles across on the other side of the room, Funcho carrying his Beta camera. We'd been separated during the flight because Funcho, wanting to smoke (this being one of the last years that was allowed on airplanes), had gone to the back. Charles, his sound recordist, followed. That left me beside a businessman on his way, ultimately, to France, who had promptly fallen asleep. I felt a twinge of annoyance. Funcho was the only one among us who spoke Portuguese; what if I needed some translation? The three of us had known each other the grand sum of three days, yet a kind of dependency had developed. I inserted myself into a ragged queue of arriving passengers, all of us pushing our bags in front of us. What Customs would turn out to be was far from clear. When I'd arrived in Harare days earlier, there had been proper desks and windows with grills, in short, a system (Zimbabwe, as I've already mentioned, had not yet then fallen apart). But this seemed pretty much a free-for-all. Quickly, I realized that the job of immigration inspection was being carried out by soldiers and soon I found myself in front of one who turned out to be not so much a proper soldier as a heavily armed boy. An adolescent, possibly no more than fifteen years old, he had a bulky Kalashnikov slung across his shoulders and a dusty face sweating under a wool beret. His face was pudgy and marked by pimples that would eventually leave his countenance pocked for life. I handed over my papers and a small bundle of US dollars, praying all would be in order. He grasped my offering with short, service-able fingers; at his wrist glistened a thin bracelet made of hammered copper. I could sense him eying my cameras, the Nikon hung around my neck, heavy against my chest, and the Canon in its case on top of my kit. He frowned and the Kalashnikov shifted on his shoulder, sending off a whiff of oil, sharp and metallic.

The young soldier unfolded my visa, a densely typed page of rigamarole in Portuguese and English that, only after a lengthy preamble, got around to the important bits, stating the name of my employer, listing my occupa-tion as a journalist, and specifying that I would be permitted to stay for up to ninety days. His brow knitted. Across the room, through the murk, I could see that Funcho and Charles had successfully made it through and were engaged in lively conversation with a tall white man, undoubt-edly our contact. I was relieved. From North America I'd never been able, through repeated attempts by both phone and letter, to make direct connection, yet here he was. That was encouraging. I looked back at the boy, who seemed engrossed in some troubling difficulty. Emboldened, I stepped forward. Despite having not a word of Portuguese, perhaps I could help. He pulled back. We were inches apart and I could smell the dust from his woolly beret, accompanied by a rolling whiff of ancient perspiration. Peremptorily, I reached as if to take the paper. He recoiled. In the split second before he folded up the paper I was able to see, with a kind of sinking dismay, that he had been studying the document with its jumble of words and official crests upside down. Our eyes connected. Puffing himself up to his full five and a half feet, he flung his head back imperiously and handed me my papers. *"Obrigado,"* I murmured, wrestling my luggage to my shoulder and moving off as quickly as I could.

Our contact· was another Canadian, which meant that none of us was from Angola. Funcho, a gleeful fellow with the odd mix of Japanese and Portuguese parentage, had been hired from Maputo, where he had once served as the personal cameraman for the president of Mozambique. Charles was the only sound recordist I'd ever met who was a member of Zimbabwe's Ndebele people and had never been to Angola before, either. Lee Ellis, who had brought his big agency 4x4 van to pick us up, had arrived five years earlier from Edmonton to direct a project providing wells and water pipes to the shantytowns that were springing up like weeds on the hillsides around the city, filled with refugees from the countryside who were fleeing the war. His interest was to get the word out through whatever method, including the television documentary and photographic articles we were set to produce, about how desperate the situation was for people he worked with—disease and overcrowding were rife—and how much foreign money would be needed to reconstruct the country. Lee had a Bulgarian wife he'd met a couple of years earlier through the foreign aid contingent and they had an apartment in the most secure segment of the city. He was paid by his Canadian agency and had perfected that quick-study expertise of the resident outsider, armed with statistics and data and political reconnaissance. His opinion seemed to be that after many false starts over the years, peace this time was finally a serious proposition and the elections being planned might put a final seal on what, at that point, had been more than twenty years of violence. Still, when he drove us through the darkened city, it was hard to know what to think.

For someone who'd come from the relative order of North America, everything I saw around me was appalling. Wrecked vehicles, many of them military, lay everywhere. At the main urban juncture we passed two hotels that at one time must have been the residence of choice for the domestic political elite and foreign businessmen. They were standard corporate design, the universally recognized pedigree for comfort, prestige, and, in this case, an imitation of another world. But there were no longer any front doors. Through the gaping openings I could see that the steps and lobbies had been taken over by men wearing bandanas and carrying automatic weapons in a parody of the way businessmen carry briefcases. Lee drove on. "I've arranged a place for you that ought to be quite secure," he said, trying to sound reassuring. Presently he turned into the courtyard of a small hostel tucked discreetly behind a secure wall and with its own guards. The place was run by a Dutch trading company and there we were going to be ensconced amongst ruddy-faced blond men representing Phillips Electronics and Heinecken beer. For the next few days we would get seven kinds of cheese and salami for breakfast and would even have television to watch: Portuguese-language soap operas from Brazil, Marxist lectures, and panel discussions on the future of maize.

From studying the map, I knew that Luanda was a port built around a decent harbour. The Portuguese had constructed the city not as the capital for their colony, but as the gritty nexus of sea traffic and connection to the outer world. The capital they dreamed of was inland, Nova Lisboa, now called Huambo and a place we were hoping to see within days. Luanda was where colonials and supplies came in and product went out, including, for a couple of centuries, vast numbers of slaves, between nine million and thirteen million, depending on whose estimates. To the south, just out of town, was a museum, prime among its artefacts a stone chair in front of which the myriads of miserable, frightened souls had been hastily baptized by some severe Jesuit before being chained into the ships. On the trip across the Atlantic, three quarters of them would die. Now, however, Luanda was the seat of government because it was held by the socialist MPLA (Movement Popular for the Liberation of Angola), the party with sufficient power to be widely recognized, most importantly by the international community, as the de facto ruler of the country. It was a garrison centre of power, the ceasefire notwithstanding; the country beyond the city margins, Lee explained, was bitterly divided, the parts east and south solidly held by the opposition Unita (National Union for the Total Independence of Angola). Lee himself seemed to sympathize with the MPLA. As a disaffected Canadian with his Bulgarian wife, he leaned naturally in the socialist direction. When the other side, Unita, was mentioned, a tick of tension would tighten his face. The opposition in both politics and war were thugs, he suggested, financed and supported by South Africa, pre-Nelson Mandela, and by Reagan-era America. Unita functionaries drove around in General Motors Corporation Jimmys and continued to pay for their considerable armaments with stolen diamonds. The MPLA, by contrast, had depended on Cuba and the Soviet Union when things were at their worst, and rode in Ladas. For money, they had access now to the sizable offshore oil reserves. From the harbour we could see the oil derricks and platforms out in the Atlantic.

Luanda, though I'd read that it was once considered one of the most beautiful cities south of the Sahara, was not to my eyes a handsome capital. It had been built for perhaps 50,000 people but, due to the influx of refugees, had swollen now to thirty times that, about a million and a half, 90% of them in hillside shantytowns. What may have once been a tidy coastal city with European-style buildings of an Iberian bent was now a wreckage. Violence, overcrowding, and general lack of upkeep had all, in their turn, contributed their bit. The streets were littered with the carcasses of wrecked vehicles, the sidewalks loaded with rubble. Debris and garbage lay everywhere. It seemed, perhaps understandably, that people had stopped bothering to clean up, knowing it was useless when another bomb was going to make a mess of their effort anyway. The ocean and semi-tropical climate might have made the place feel Mediterranean, like Marseilles or Nice, but it looked more like Haiti. The trees and the boulevards were naked.

My immediate reaction to all this was to not sleep. The second, third, fourth night I'd fall on my bed and then just lie there, my brain refusing to give up whatever it needed to allow me to enter the elusive zone. The way I saw it, I'd landed somewhere new and my body decided to rebel. Human evolution might someday get us to the place where we can cope smoothly as we leap across time zones and parachute into the stresses of new environments, but it hasn't yet. I tossed and turned and tried to get comfortable. I would attempt to halt the roil of images and thoughts by willing my mind, through intense focus, to go blank, a white screen. Never succeeding in this, of course, I would inevitably veer to another tack, willing myself to think about purely mechanical things like naming the countries of South

America south to north and then the states of America from west to east. From time to time this would almost work but not quite; abruptly I would be back, screamingly alert and more irritated by the minute. I experimented with everything: masturbation, ever since I was fourteen years old, had been a standard ploy. I tried that, yet remained as awake as ever. I fumbled for my watch but the lighted digits seemed irrelevant; due to all the time zone changes of the recent week, I had no idea what the hour was supposed to be. When I did manage to drift off, it was to sail straightaway into a ghoulish roil of nightmares, including having the boy at the airport chase me through endless corridors brandishing his gun. At dawn I woke in a sweat, more exhausted than ever.

The first morning when I came down to breakfast, Funcho and I took a look at one another and he started to laugh. We had on identical photographer's vests. "Banana Republic store Fifth Avenue New York City," he exclaimed, fumbling for a cigarette and stepping over to finger the material of my garment. "I got mine when I was filming the president of Mozambique at the UN," he said. I hadn't purchased mine in New York, but it was the same brand: thirty-six-pocket version. You could carry everything from notebooks to rolls of film to your lunch, besides the fact that there were secret compartments hidden away in hard-to-locate corners where money and passports could be stowed. A robber or pickpocket would have to kill you to get at the valuables. But beyond their practicality, our outfits served another purpose: they were uniforms that declared, as surely as did any military uniform or police officer's uniform, businessman's fine suit, or jersey of a team athlete, "I have a right to be here." It would be impossible to overemphasize how desperately important that purpose seemed at the moment; we both realized how much we needed to reassure ourselves that we could be where we were.

On our second morning we lugged our equipment into Lee's van— Funcho his Betacam, Charles his recording gear, me my cameras just in case. We weren't actually sure when we were starting work; it was all work. A few minutes earlier, I had initiated a meeting to discuss our 'mission'. Funcho fiddled with his camera and Lee sprawled on the sofa in the corner of the lounge. The producer booking us back in Toronto had been explicit: in exchange for access through various officials already on the ground and people like Lee, we were to come back with a documentary that would explain the work being done in a difficult situation by the agencies we were scheduled to visit. All of them were clients of the UN and various Western governments that (no small matter) were also providing the money to pay us. The responsibility was clear-cut and solemn, but while such a mandate made things easier, it also carried its own built-in trouble. I looked to the others, worried they might think we were going to turn out something like advertising rather than the objective journalism we all professed to respect. I particularly watched Funcho, who was a hardbitten veteran who had worked all over the place for all sorts of clients, including German TV. The tape he'd offered to his prospective employers for this trip included footage from a hair-raising ride in an open railway boxcar while being fired at by Mozambican rebels. As for Charles, I had no idea what he might be thinking; whenever he spoke it was with a voice so soft you could hardly discern what he was saying. But hearkening back to discussions that had seemed to make so much sense when held in comfortable offices on the other side of the world, I ploughed on: the warring sides in the country were locked into a ceasefire, elections had been called, foreign monitors were already on the ground with more arriving every week. It was set to be an historic moment. "We're supposed to find," I said, reiterating the mandate given me by our producers, "the signs of hope."

We set off. The immediate vicinity around our compound was acceptably secure. Now we were going to be taken through the broad expanse of the city. Lee announced that we were headed toward a market that he guaranteed would be unlike anything any of us, even Charles and Funcho, would have ever seen. I could tell he hoped to shock us and was relishing the opportunity to develop a little suspense. Now that we'd had a couple of days under his guidance, I was becoming more impressed at each turn by the sang-froid required for the Canadian simply to carry out his daily life here. He lived with a certain calm in an environment that was anything but calm.

The signs we were approaching something substantial came early. Most people were far too poor to have cars and the city in general was thin of traffic. Suddenly, however, we were mired in a maze of snarled automobiles, carts, and people on foot. Crawling against a cacophony of noise and a haze of fumes, we inched forward until, turning a corner, we were faced with our destination, an entire hillside covered with people, like proverbial ants. It took a few minutes to absorb the magnitude of it all. Lee was right, it was not a market in any simple sense, but the biggest configuration of buyers and sellers any of us had ever seen, every square foot of packed dirt occupied. The driver stopped so we could take it in with proper respect. Funcho hoisted his Betacam to his shoulder, pushed the lens through the open window, and began a slow pan. By focusing my eye and then my camera, I determined that everything from pots to bananas to bedroom suites were for sale from impromptu plots staked out on the ground or out of the backs of lorries. It was like forty Wal-Marts. Thousands, perhaps tens of thousands, of people either with something to sell or wanting to buy.

The scene was both panoramic and immediate. It kaleidoscoped infinitely until it disappeared into a distant and indistinct haze, but we could also focus it sharply right in front of our noses. Our presence made us a mild object of curiosity. But mild only, and local. People were much more intent on securing a deal on a plastic pail or a couple of plantains than reacting to a vehicle full of foreigners. As well, in a country accustomed to more than its share of uncertainty, including the constant movement of soldiers and mercenaries and foreigners of various stripes, one more vanload seemed not so special. A bunch of kids, about six of them in ragged T-shirts, started to ham for the cameras, which they spotted right away. Then they began to try to wheedle some change. "Don't give any out," advised Lee, "or we'll have a thousand of them on us. Keep moving," he ordered the driver. He shouted something in Portuguese at the urchins, who promptly, looking spiteful, scampered away.

We rolled haltingly forward, lurching, unavoidably for the poor driver, into a pothole, which caused Funcho and his camera to crash against the door. "You have to stop," he said. "I have to get out."

"It's dangerous," warned Lee.

"Guard my back," said Funcho.

Charles gathered his microphones and followed into the fray. I might have preferred to remain in the van but couldn't very well now that the ante had been raised. I grasped the Canon and my small bag. Once out, I felt decidedly liberated. I knew I should stay close to Funcho and Charles, perhaps even play some role as their guard. But the scenes before me were extraordinary. I looked back. Lee had emerged from the van in a tentative gesture and stood beside it, a deep frown on his face. I took a step toward a woman holding up a leg of raw meat, possibly goat, whose blanket of angry flies buzzed away as she shook it. I waited out the whirr of my film advancing. Everything I could see through my viewfinder or hear coming into my ears or smell—the horrible, heavy, wafting odours of charcoal smoke and rapidly decaying food and fumes from badly tuned engines— was both fascinating and offensive. Which was my dilemma. I wanted to get past my revulsion and wade into the world that lay in front of me, but I couldn't. This grand scene had to have its own logic, but I couldn't find it. To me it came across only as chaos. Even though I was standing right on the ground in the middle of it, I felt like I was looking in from some impossibly faraway vantage point. I wasn't in any way part of this. I was alien, removed, superfluous; this had started without me and would go on without me. I neither caused it, affected its workings, or benefited from it. I was, that worst of all terms, irrelevant.

When we clambered back into the vehicle, I could tell Lee was pleased with himself. We left the scene and, after a good deal of careful manoeuvring on the part of the driver, were able to wend our way once again into the city proper. We drove past—and I tried to photograph—monuments: an unfinished one to the first socialist president, Agostinho Neto, who had been dead almost a dozen years, and others put together from artillery guns mounted precariously on pedestals. Lee instructed the driver to make a turn and soon we were on a route that led down along the shore. We crested a small hill, and eventually pulled up and parked in front of a sprawling hotel. This, suddenly, was a completely different world. It might have been in Hawaii, so different was it from the other places we'd seen. Even the name of the hotel, The Panorama, was expansive. Palm trees waved in front and it seemed undamaged by either war or hooliganism. Across the road was the Atlantic Ocean, shimmering in the midday sun with fishermen sorting their nets, women carrying the last pails of the catch toward braziers set up further along on the beach, and kids running in circles. After the two hours we'd just spent in the hectic chaos of the market, this was like coming into a calm bay after a storm. We took the concrete steps up toward a terrace, which overlooked both the beach and a thick grove of tropical trees and flowers, a protected park. The breeze was pleasant and the sun warm. We took a table right in the sun in the middle of the terrace and ordered German mineral water. Around us was an assembly thoroughly unlike what we'd so far encountered in this country. Lee smiled purposefully. This, we could tell without his having to say anything, was the upper-end version of what we'd just witnessed at the outdoor market: the new economy, opportunity taking hold. Two men in dark suits huddled around a bottle of vodka and cups of coffee with a third man, a soldier, an army general in spotless green fatigues and sparkling ribbons. Lee, with a furtive nod, whispered that the two men in suits were cabinet ministers. Three women dripping diamonds and gold jewellery waited at the next table, looking exceedingly bored. Maybe they were wives, or maybe they were hookers; either way, they waited for the men who had supplied the diamonds and the gold jewellery. One of them stirred her coffee with the long lacquered nail of her pinky finger. Beyond the low wall of the terrace, I noted sleek Mercedeses idling in the parking lot, watched by men who could have been bodyguards for Mike Tyson. The tallest of the three women looked over and smiled. The table on the other side of us was taken by a short man with a gigantic briefcase, the contents of which were soon laid out around him. Birds screeched. On the horizon a floating oil derrick lay at anchor. Funcho, who had been taking in the scene with some cagey calculation, leaned in on our table. "We should film these people," he pronounced in a low voice, looking first to Lee and then to me for reaction. "They seem hopeful."

2

HUAMBO

THE TOWN OF HUAMBO WAS AS DIFFERENT from Luanda as Manchester might be from London or Saskatoon from Vancouver. It lay deep inside the country, almost inaccessible, thanks to ruined roads and a destroyed rail line, although we were able to make it a mere hop of an hour and a half in a small plane Lee had hired from an American-based Christian mission group. In the midst of even the worst chaos, such luxuries are possible if you have connections and money—in an odd way, even more possible than in better functioning societies or circumstances. The Beechcraft King Air had two single rows of seats so everybody had a window and, since we were flying low, it was possible to take everything in. On the brilliantly clear day it was like watching a movie, a vast, rolling carpet of open spaces, forests, and plateaux I knew to be wealthy in minerals, water, arable soil, timber. The landscape was movingly beautiful, verdant and, certainly from the height we were at, nearly empty. Angola is twice as big as France but with only ten million people, at that time, thinly populated in relative terms. I thought about this. I also considered how hard it was to fathom that, down below, so much had been destroyed and that war and mostly politics had been allowed to change things so radically. Looking at the world from the air is a lot like studying a map, everything ordered and stable and peaceful, but down below it would all be different. Huambo, Lee had warned, would show us infinitely more war damage than Luanda.

We were happy to leave Luanda. Moving on in any travel situation always offers hope for at least the brief period until you find out how bad things are in the new place. At the airport, while we waited for our little private plane to be brought around, I asked a worker to point me to a toilet. He looked at me quizzically, not quite understanding my Portuguese, then his face brightened in a grin both cynical and joyous. He waved his arm in a loopy circle: go where you like, it was all a toilet. I stepped carefully behind an outside wall and spied, almost immediately, movement out of the corner of my eye. A couple of young men, naked to the waist, were firing boxes over the fence. They were looting somebody's recent arrival of cargo goods and doing so in broad daylight. At the far end of the runways, waiting to rust or be stripped of whatever removable parts they had, sat hulking old Russian planes from Aeroflot.

Once on the ground, we needed a place to stay. Lee had arranged a hotel in the middle of town and we carried our luggage into the lobby. It was dreadful, desolate and dark as if no light bulb had been turned on in it for twenty years, which was possibly the case. Four skinny men in shiny suits huddled fussily in the gloom around the check-in desk, as if to give the impression no hotel on earth was better staffed. But the room they offered showed no indication of having been cleaned within the decade. The bed sagged, the single sheet was yellow and stained, the blanket smelled of many bodies. After the Dutch place in Luanda, this was a rude shock. The bathroom was spacious with all the facilities, including a bidet. But the porcelain was stained with rust and all the chrome blistered and rough. And the coup de grace, there was no water. It was nice modern design but the problem was that modern worked only when it worked. When things faltered, as they unmistakably had here for going on twenty years, modern could equate to horrid. Much better to be in a grass hut with a biffy in the nearby jungle. I returned to the lobby and could tell that Funcho and Charles, having seen their quarters, felt the same way. Lee frowned. He seemed miffed that we didn't approve of his choice. "Well," he said archly, "there only is one other hotel. If you don't like this one, go have a look at it." The four men behind the desk looked bewildered. Lee appeared determined to stay where he was, but Funcho and Charles didn't waste a moment taking up his challenge and I followed them out the door. We crossed the street to a simpler spot, which likewise had neither electricity nor water, but somehow seemed cheerier and, stripped of pretensions, more acceptable than the place that still pretended that two decades of civil war had made no difference in their level of service. The room here had no glass in the window, but that meant an abundance of fresh air and I liked that. We booked in. Five US dollars a night. Then we went back, feeling like we had to make things up, and shared a meal of rice and stringy beef—the beef so dark it was almost black—with Lee in the dingy restaurant of the first hotel.

The whole of the town pretty much took its cue from our two hotels; Lee was right, this place had sustained infinitely more damage than Luanda. For the travelling Westerner, there is something comforting wherever he finds European architecture and Huambo had an abundance of it. The Portuguese colonials had planned and spent lavishly. But it was all crumbling. Stories abounded that those same Portuguese colonials, when fleeing, had said their good-byes by pouring concrete into the service mains. Since then nothing had happened except shelling and the deterioration that is inevitable from neglect and lack of resources. My room on the fourth floor, for example, had a bathroom with four services—sink, toilet, bathtub, and bidet—but there had been no water for perhaps ten years. The building had an elevator, as well—which didn't work. Yet, the chambermaid, a slender young woman named Esmerelda, supplied me each morning with enough water, if I planned everything properly, to shave, brush my teeth, and have a sort of stand-up bath, pouring some of the water, shower-style, over my head to wash my hair. When that was all completed, I could dump the remainder down the toilet to achieve a flush—the drains, apparently, still worked. The water, about four gallons of it (cold), arrived in a red plastic tub carried up the four flights of narrow stairs—which replaced the non-functioning elevator—on Esmerelda's head. What affects the traveller most directly is his own lodgings, both for what they provide, or fail to, for comfort and security, but also as the most immediate yardstick with which to assess the material situation of the entire community. Our documentary-making task was to take note of the deprivations and destructions in this country; our hotels and rooms put those as close as our own skin.

In the midst of it, the people of Huambo seemed eager to communicate with the outside world. Some months earlier, a BBC crew had been there and another was expected some weeks in the future. But by and large, few outsiders had ever come here to listen to what people had to say or attempt to carry their stories back out. With the Soviet Union collapsed and the Cold War ended, any geopolitical strategic importance for Angola as a whole had evaporated and, to much of the outside world, it had slipped precipitously into the realm of yet one more faraway African country mired in chaos. Who could make head or tail of it? Who wanted to? So, armed with our television camera and assorted other paraphernalia and intentions, our welcome in Huambo was assured, much more than in Luanda. We had but to remain open to their stories and the people of Huambo would impart them to us. Lee, as well, had done his work. Two local officials wanted to meet us right off, both of them substantial figures: the governor of the district and a sixty-two-year-old clergyman named Reverend Julio Francisco.

The governor might have seemed the more important on the face of things, but in the long run the more formidable institution, the one that had both the people and the staying power, was Pastor Julio's church. The Catholic Church, though it functioned throughout the country, had been handicapped because of having come hand-in-hand with Portuguese colonialism. After four centuries, it continued to be burdened by the skepticism of large numbers of the people. But American Protestants had also done missionary work and in Huambo the fruits of their efforts were much in evidence. This was a Christian town in practice as well as designation, with the church one of the more enduring and respected institutions. On a Sunday morning you could hear singing from any of a number of churches from three blocks away. At the core of this Protestant Church was Pastor Julio. He was a quick, bird-like man with darting eyes behind heavily framed glasses and a pinched face that would explode, when he smiled, into a bright pie pan. He was dressed, always, in an impeccable dark grey suit and colourful tie as if he was, somehow, an urbane executive he'd seen on his trips to America rather than a preacher in a virtually inaccessible corner of Africa. The pastor's local following was huge, and his connections to America, even through the worst moments of the war, had never fractured. With aid dollars that filtered through, he had managed to maintain schools and clinics that were parallel to, and in many cases replaced, those of the government. Nationalistic and fiercely independent, he had required, through everything, discipline and citizenship from his people. And now as the country lurched into its present moment of ceasefire and portended elections, Pastor Julio claimed, as well, to be in charge of hope. "You have come at the most exciting of times," he greeted us enthusiastically. "We are ready for peace. The people are hopeful that their lives will at last be set right." It was impossible not to want to wish him well.

On Sunday afternoon at 1:45 sharp the pastor arrived to fetch us for our visit to the governor. He had a shiny new four-wheel-drive Toyota Land Cruiser capable of seating eight, complete with a driver, an attractive young woman named Dorta, who turned out to be his niece and, with a good command of English, doubled as his translator. In Huambo nothing was far from anything else. From the hotels we proceeded up a short street, which turned to pass the train station and railway yards. A once smart-looking building with a whitewashed facade and a long covered platform adorned with ironwork, the station had been the centre of all action, gathering not only passengers but the substantial agricultural product of the countryside and sending it down to the coast. Now it was a mess: broken windows and a sagging roof on the building, ruined carriages and boxcars, locomotives rusting and stripped of parts, weeds growing up between the ties and the tracks.

In Huambo something else was certainly more visible than in Luanda. Amputees. What I'd seen a bit in the capital here appeared epidemic. Everywhere were people hopping on one leg or all too often with no legs at all. Dorta swerved to avoid a young man struggling across the road. He was possibly twenty-five years old and had one leg of his trousers folded and pinned above where his right knee should have been. He manoeuvred with some agility, working a set of shiny aluminium crutches, the kind you grip at the wrist. Others who lined the sides of the dusty road had cruder instruments, often just branches cut from trees. "These people step on mines when they are chasing their cow," Pastor Julio offered, clucking his tongue and shaking his head.

Added Dorta, "The cows are frequently blown up too."

Most of the amputees appeared to be young men but there was a fair number of women and even children among the casualties as well. The whole country was a minefield, a lethal trap where going for a walk could spell the end of you, and explosives, placed by both sides, had made the rail line and many roads inoperable and had likewise demolished a considerable number of people. Thirty thousand amputees, Lee told us, was the common estimate. On top of that, of course, were the numbers of those who didn't live to become amputees. Anybody unfortunate enough to have lost both legs was mired in particular difficulty; proper wheelchairs were rare. More commonly we encountered these people pushing along on crude contraptions that looked like skateboards or the dollies you'd use to move a refrigerator, barely clearing the ground, their tiny wheels lurching on every bump and into every crevice. The loss of limbs, the most obvious of wounds, was a dismaying sight. Later we would visit and film a Red Cross centre where prosthetics were manufactured and fitted; the most booming industry in the town. And the effect was going to be felt for a long time. "The number of land mines that will remain in this country, even after peace," declared the pastor, "is a terrible thing."

Lee jumped in with the number: "Perhaps a million."

I realized that people who live with war, who know nothing else, exist completely outside all my conceptions. The question of 'normal' is a significant one. If my country, Canada, were to be at war, I'd be able to cope with it only by thinking of it as a temporary situation during which we would have to hold our breath. A large conflict would be unfathomable, and even a small one could be seen only as a vast aberration interrupting the life we know and like. What would happen to the hockey season? Summer holidays? The school year? The stock market? It is not just the violence and fear, but a derailing of all the markers of life as we know it. When I used to listen as a child to my parents and grandparents discussing World War II, I was left with images of a crisis that gained the entire culture's attention. That war was far away but, because our country was involved, it was likewise immediate. People from every family had gone away to fight in it, the local economy was geared to supplying it. It was psychically draining and needed, therefore, to be seen as passing. By and large, we do not have the mental stamina to last long other than in the state of normalcy that we believe we deserve; anything else is an aberration, like a storm that knocks down your trees and forces you to hide in the cellar.

But for people here, the hostilities had been both immediate and persistent. The brief version of the recent history of Angola begins with an uprising of workers on cotton and coffee plantations in the country's most northerly province in 1961. In skirmishes and terror hits, 400 Portuguese settlers were killed. The colonists retaliated with reprisals of the most brutal sort, which left 40,000 black Angolans dead. Targeted specifically were the fledgling intelligentsia, the tiny few who had gained literacy and then found themselves designated "carriers of the infections of nationalism." The war to gain independence continued, sporadic and cruel, until 1974, blossoming into success only—and suddenly—when a coup in Lisbon overthrew the long-standing Salazar regime. But there was no holiday from violence in Angola. Immediately, the independence parties—there were several of them, three main ones[1]—took their struggle for control of the new country into conflict with one another; what had been a war to end colonialism became a fratricidal civil war, tribal in some sense but also party-based, ideological, and driven by egotistical future dictators meddled with by far-off superpowers and their CIA and KGB agents.

This is all far too common as an African story of the late twentieth century. Parallels of Angola's story can be found in any number of neighbouring countries, no matter who their former colonial masters. French, Belgian, English, Portuguese, it was all the same, colonialism's yoke thrown off in struggles where the best and the brightest first return from a European education and then find themselves in local prisons. Mandela, Kenyatta, Lumumba. Those who believe themselves freedom fighters are designated

by the local powers as terrorists. In response to the first sporadic acts of defiance, reprisals are doled out ten to one, or a hundred to one. But ultimately
the edifice crumbles, only to be followed then by the civil war, many more
deaths, and the planting of seeds of enduring bitterness. Eventually (though
it hadn't happened in Angola yet) somebody wins and sets himself up as a
dictator, followed fast on his heels by corruption on a mind-boggling scale.
Then the lengthy struggle of the new nations to climb out of the hole, out
of the mess, new battles necessitated against the World Bank and the plays
of global geopolitics for oil and minerals, gambits seeking to rob every bit
as much local wealth as the slave traders and ivory hunters ever did. How
many countries can we count throughout the continent of Africa where
this has been the story? And how will it all turn out?

By the time we arrived in 1992, Angola's conflicts had been going on
for so long that people we saw on the street, all those with their missing
limbs, had known no other life but uncertainty, violence, and paralysis of the
economic potential of the country and its culture. Loss, fear, anxiety, if not
"normal," were at least accepted to a far greater degree than I would have
been able to accept them. On the mantel in Pastor Julio's house sat a framed
photograph of a young man clutching a diploma and looking as if all the
whole world ought to be his for the asking: the school graduation photo
of the pastor's son, killed in 1979. Pastor Julio, Dorta, the young governor
we were about to meet, Esmerelda the chambermaid, and the amputees
on the street, when they went to sleep, when they awakened, when they
courted, when they made love, when they planted their gardens or their
crops and when they were lucky enough to harvest them, had to do so
inside a climate of ever-present potential of disaster. Daily life consisted of a
landmine spotted only in the nick of time—or not—a bombed railway car,
a ruined road, a field too dangerous to plant, a cow pasture with landmines
on the trail. When the armies came, they trampled your crops, butchered
your cow for their supper, raped your sister. All of life was proscribed by
this, both joy and suffering. Dorta, bright and personable and intelligent,
had managed to get out of the country to study sociology at a university in Brazil, but she had returned. She had a boyfriend she was slated to
marry; she would marry, she told us, and have children. If things went as

everybody desperately wanted, the expected peace would provide a new and more secure context. But she would have done the same at any other time in thirty years, what else could she do? My colleagues, I felt, might understand—Funcho had lived through a similar period in Mozambique (though his father, a landowner and Portuguese, would have been on the other side); Charles was the child of parents who had survived both the independence war and the civil war as Rhodesia became Zimbabwe. These people understood that this was life, you couldn't stop and wait for it to pass, it was what was. Yet, while they might accept it, for me to do so was so difficult as to be virtually impossible.

The governor's mansion was a white, porticoed structure straight out of South Carolina. We turned off the littered, ramshackle street and approached on a curving driveway through guarded gates. We parked our vehicle next to riotous flower beds, and then were escorted past a couple of stern-faced soldiers in immaculate garb into a spacious anteroom with nicely tiled floors. Minutes later, a young man of about thirty-five with a beefy body and a pleasant, round face entered, dressed in creased trousers and a luminous white shirt. Gustavo Balthasar's proper title turned out to be vice-governor, which was not actually an underling position because he was the chief local administrator and underling only to the central government in Luanda. He shook hands all around, pausing as Pastor Julio made my introduction using more words than he had for the others. I looked to Dorta for translation. "Chief of our delegation," she said. This seemed a bit extravagant but I offered my hand. We'd agreed in advance that this would be a courtesy call only, a diplomatic visit, if you will; we wouldn't set up for an interview on camera. In short order I regretted this. No sooner had we got settled in a salon furnished with French Provincial-style settees, sipping politely on tea and munching cookies, when Senor Balthasar dropped a bombshell. He didn't believe that he would last the year, he confided matter-of-factly; he expected to be assassinated. He told us this in English and I glanced quickly at Lee and then to see if Dorta would translate for Pastor Julio. "Democracy," he said, "would have to be more than one election." But he was pessimistic that even one would go well. And if it didn't, or if it didn't for his party, then he believed that he too would be finished. Perhaps literally.

As with Pastor Julio and his church, the vice-governor had US connections. Not many months before, he had been a student at Temple University in Pennsylvania at work on a Master's program in economics. But when his political associates issued the call to come home, he felt he had no choice. He was MPLA and the party offered him the governorship here in Huambo. The reason for his anxiety was that it was not a posting with guaranteed safety. As Lee had pointed out numerous times, this was primarily Unita country—even Pastor Julio's allegiance was possibly in that direction. Recognizing this, our young host had left his wife and three children in Philadelphia. "At least until after the elections," he said mournfully.

The Toyota Land Cruiser was a godsend. It was big enough to accommodate both us and our equipment with ease, as well as high off the ground and rugged enough to handle the muddy roads, pocked as they were with landmine craters. I don't know if money changed hands between Lee and the pastor, I hope it did, but at any rate for the next few days, this fine vehicle along with the helpful, cheerful Dorta was going to be at our disposal. The next morning, we waited with our gear on the road in front of the hotel. Television field gear has seen a revolution in size. With each generation of innovation, it has become more and more compact so that it now can be easily packed by a single operator. At that time, although we believed we were travelling as light as we could, we still had a Betacam camera at about twenty kilograms, assorted cases of microphones and wires, a box of tapes, and a carton of heavy batteries to power it all. As well, we had a boom pole, two tripods, and my bag of cameras, notebooks, and so on. When the big white vehicle rounded the corner, we were happy to see it.

However, before it rolled to a stop, I realized there wasn't nearly as much room as we had been expecting. Dorta and Pastor Julio weren't alone. Though we liked to think we and our mission were the priority, every once in a while we were reminded that wasn't entirely the case. Inside with Pastor Julio, dressed up in their Sunday best, was an entire cadre of his friends, other pastors. As the van came to a stop, Lee rolled his eyes. "Good god," he breathed. The pastors, however, were in a very good mood. *"Bom dia,"* they smiled broadly, *"bom dia."* They all reached to shake our hands. We were scheduled to make a trip of about two hours' distance into the countryside to see a once-important (but now destroyed) mission village. Since this was a place close to their hearts that none of them would have been able to visit perhaps for years, it was hard to blame them for wanting to come along. Lee paced in a big circle, trying to put a cork in his irritation, then came back and started talking in Portuguese to Pastor Julio. Funcho looked angry. In the end Lee threw up his hands; the pastors were all going to come along. I took a careful look and figured that if we really squeezed, we could manage it. Funcho with his camera took the front seat across from Dorta. Charles got in behind him so they could be connected for any through-the-window shooting. I got the pastors to help load our equipment, making them at least a little bit useful, and then we climbed over one another into the back, squeezing ourselves like sardines.

Once out of town, I began to see the reality of the situation. Even in our cramped state, we were better off than anybody we were encountering. Most other people were either walking or on bicycles; every other vehicle was an IFA truck belching smoke or an old Peugeot held together with wire. I felt bad about our little fit of pique and hoped the pastors wouldn't consider us as ungracious as we, in fact, had been. A lorry snorting diesel fumes lumbered along, its open box jammed with what might easily have been fifty people, all of them standing up. Nothing but faces looking out overtop of the racks. Beside the road, the produce of the country moved not on trucks but on the heads of women who walked, barefoot, in a seemingly endless parade. The women carried everything: long sticks for firewood, pots, burlap sacks filled with charcoal, maize, or whatever, even bulky bales of hay, which could be four times the size of the carrier herself. One very skinny woman in a ragged dress had tools, an axe and a shovel, handles forward, carefully balanced. Many, along with their other load, had babies, most slung on their backs except for those who carried two and then had to have them both front and back. Every one of these women had such grace of carriage she could have been instantly auditioned by any ballet company in the world, but here they were the poorest of the poor, serene and stolid-faced while functioning as pack animals.

Though we were going only about eighty kilometres, the trip took almost three hours. Once, we stopped to help about forty other people pushing a big IFA truck stuck in the mud. Finally we arrived at and turned down a hardly used trail. As if they were entering some sacred space, the pastors all went silent. The mission village was called Donde, and when it appeared around a turn in the trail, it was like a mediaeval ruin, nothing but brick walls and archways left of something that at one time could have resembled Yale University. The weeds growing up between the walls now under the open sky were shoulder-high. We stopped and the pastors stepped gingerly out of the vehicle, trooping off for a reverent wander around while Funcho set up his camera. "This," said Pastor Julio, walking through knee-high grass by a tumbled wall and some twisted girders, "was the classrooms." When he was a boy, Pastor Julio had been a resident here, as had a number of the others, taught by American and Canadian mission-aries. One notable fellow student, he said, was now off in the bush as leader of the Unita rebels: Jonas Savimbi. The pastor remembered him as a "good student" but diplomatically withheld comment on his role as architect of so much of Angola's current troubles. The school complex, including teachers' houses and offices, which were now just empty shells occupying the next hill, had been hit early in the wars. A fire, shelling, looting, vandalism all in turn had done their work. Slogans and propaganda graffiti painted on the brick told some of the story. The MPLA and their Cuban allies had arrived first, covering over pictures of the Christian saints and Jesus Christ himself with a gigantic portrait of Karl Marx and hammer and sickle emblems. Then Unita had tried to paint them out, not succeeding entirely. Alas, all was left now to the grass and the birds and the intense, mournful, soughing wind.

We climbed back into the Toyota for a short drive to what had been another part of the complex, a clinic and infirmary. It was becoming mid-afternoon and beginning to sprinkle rain. The medical quarter turned out to be another wreckage, except that a few of the buildings, one-storey constructions, were at least partially covered over with roofing.

Astonishingly, under this tenuous shelter, ragged figures huddled around charcoal fires. A few more stood in doorways. Since everything else had been so deserted, to find these people was a bit of a shock. A man in a white smock emerged and marched over to greet us, seemingly overjoyed to encounter visitors. His name was Texiera, he said, and he was a nurse. He offered to take us through what he called "his wards." Funcho hoisted his camera, Charles put on his headphones, and we followed into a series of damp, mildewed rooms with sweating concrete floors. It was like a scene from some biblical-era plague; everywhere, people lay on pallets, some of them moaning softly, the rest silent. At our arrival they looked up, but few seemed to have either the energy or the will for anything other than a blank stare. "Malaria, AIDS, leprosy, childbirth," Texiera marched through, pointing out his caseload. There was no doctor and he and a couple of lab technicians sharing a lone microscope in a dispensary with no glass in the window were the grand sum of the staff. But for all the people on their sorry pallets, villagers from the settlements in the surrounding hills, this was it for available medical care. What money Texiera received was forwarded either by Pastor Julio, whom he acknowledged profusely, from his foreign mission sources, or arrived in dribs and drabs from the Unita political party. But there had been no money from either for some time and Texiera had been working without pay for months. Still, for the pastors, the fact that the place was functioning at all represented a kind of triumph and they smiled broadly, forcing handshakes on all the forlorn patients.

We took a few more shots, including one of the dispensary with hardly any bottles of medicine on its shelves, then packed up our cameras, feeling not a little guilty about our ability to move on. The rain started to come down more steadily and before we were even back to the main road, it was pelting, which forced Dorta to work extremely hard to keep the truck going in the increasingly slippery track. For a while it poured down in sheets and I was wishing she would pull over and wait it out. But then it stopped and the late-day sun came out. We were back on the main road by then, pulling into a town now not far from Huambo. I could hardly wait to get home. The desk clerk at the hotel sometimes kept beer, whose purchase could be negotiated, and I could already taste it. But suddenly an interchange in Portuguese went from one of the pastors to Pastor Julio to Dorta. She took an abrupt turn off the main road and pulled to a stop. The pastors jumped out. "What's going on?" Lee asked. Then, after hearing Pastor Julio's reply, he turned to us, clearly exasperated. The pastors had one more surprise for us up their sleeve. "They've arranged to have supper here," Lee said. "We apparently have no choice." Funcho lit a cigarette.

We trooped up a muddy walkway to a simple two-room house, mud brick and an asbestos sheeting roof. Surrounding it was a fence with a small garden populated by a couple of chickens scratching in the wet dirt. This had all obviously been planned ahead of time, for inside, in the main room, they were expecting us. Spread out was a long, low table with benches and chairs for everyone. A few men were already there waiting, a couple of them quite elderly. Bustling in the background, seen in flashes through a doorway where steam billowed and from which the smells of cooking food wafted, were half a dozen women. The pastors motioned us to sit down and promptly plates of food appeared: rice, stewed chicken, trays of boiled greens. Only the men, including Funcho, Charles, and I, were seated in the main room around the table. Dorta disappeared through the doorway and joined the women in the kitchen. In the room with us, watching silently from squatting positions in the corner, were a couple of young children and a dog. The pastors chattered away for a while in an amalgam of Portuguese and a tribal language, recounting, I suspected, a report of the day's trip to the old ones who had not been along. Funcho, Charles, and I dug in. The food was delicious and plentiful. No sooner would a plate be emptied than a woman would appear from the cookery with a replacement. Presently one of the old men began to talk and everyone else fell silent. Pastor Julio leaned over to me. "You want to listen to this," he said. "This man has suffered greatly. He has been put in prison by every one of the powers in Angola's conflicts. Portuguese, Unita, MPLA." The pastor looked to Lee to see if he might be able to translate but he called for Dorta, who re-emerged and took a seat among the men.

It was true. The old man, whose name was Enrico and who was seventy-eight years old, had fallen either by accident or by treachery onto the wrong side at one time or another of every actor in the wars. Three times in jail, he'd been set free only once and twice he'd managed to escape. The longest detainment had been for eighteen months, after which he arrived home to discover his entire family killed. He started again and altogether had three wives; the second had died of cholera and the third was in the kitchen just behind us, dishing out the last of the chicken stew. One of the young children watching us eat was a son from this third marriage. Enrico had a lovely face, pliable like Plasticine, and coarse grey hair the consistency of steel wool. His story came out in short, lyrical bursts, like music, with his pausing after each paragraph or so for the translation to catch up, then pushing ahead again. The others had all heard it before, this performance was for our benefit. At one point the small boy, who was about five years old, padded across the dirt floor and crawled up into his lap. Not missing a beat, the old man continued with his story, acknowledging the small boy only by folding his large hands around him, knitting his long, bony fingers together to make the cradle safe.

3

REPORTAGE

I HAD TO GIVE CHARLES AND FUNCHO SOME MONEY. Our arrangements were for fee plus expenses, but I had to agree with them that when the hotel cost only five dollars a night, I was getting off pretty easy at the expense end of things. Moreover, it was decidedly difficult to live here. At the end of a long day, the usual things weren't to be had, there was no TV to watch and no hot showers, restaurants were few and far between, much less good ones, and proper food of any sort was chancy. Ryszard Kapuscinski, the great Polish correspondent who visited nearly every hellhole on earth, has written about the boredom and loneliness of the outpost assignments and how the only friend is "whiskey, cognac, liqueurs, schnapps and beers." But, with the exception of the occasional black market stash to be had from beneath the desk of the hotel clerk, those too were difficult to obtain and unreliable. Since my colleagues were easily subsidizing the project and doing so without complaint, I needed to make it right with my wad of US dollars. My employers, recognizing there would be no reliable bank to take credit cards or even traveller's cheques, had sent me with cash, about $16,000, which I lugged everywhere in a money belt under my shirt, there rarely being any other place to safely store it. To get rid of some of it was a relief.

It wasn't that it was all difficulty. One day we went to interview the UN peacekeeping commander. While we were there, Charles encountered a fellow Zimbabwean among the supporting cast of international soldiers. That night they set off to try to find whether Huambo had any hidden delights to offer. They must have had a pretty good time because Charles didn't come back until four in the morning.

The United Nations encampment was at the southern edge of town. Back in Luanda, there was a UN headquarters where, on our return, we'd arranged to stop for one last interview with the chief civilian functionary, a British woman, the direct representative of the secretary general sent to oversee Angola's elections. Out here, the presence was a military one, not peacekeepers exactly but still soldiers from twenty-four countries with the task of keeping the two sides of the conflict away from one another until those elections took place. They called themselves a "verification unit" and they had to verify on a great number of matters. The situation was a bit like an elaborate schoolyard where the teacher has to step forward and hold scrapping parties apart, perhaps even sending them to put their heads down on their desks for half an hour. In their ceasefire signed the previous autumn, the Angolan parties had pledged to disarm and accept supervision to meld parts of each of their fighting forces into a single national army. This hand-picking of both the acceptable and the best from what had been two opposing hostile forces was going to be a time-consuming and tricky job. Then there were the soldiers who didn't go into that national army, which was most of them; they were supposed to give up their uniforms, take a small payout, and return to "normal life," which one could only hope might mean a job or a bit of schooling. The UN task was a herding and bookkeeping one; vast numbers of soldiers from both sides had to be amassed in parallel camps, housed there until some balance was achieved, relieved of their weapons, and then watched to make sure they stayed put. Both sides were finicky and hardly trusting of one another, so the UN had to function as both referee and accountant. The soldiers, we'd been told, were gathering quite readily, but street gossip also had it that for every weapon being turned in, two more were being hidden somewhere in the bush.

We went to see the UN colonel, who happened to be a Canadian. He was snappy in his blue beret and stood at attention for our entire interview, a shimmering silk cravat at his throat, the UN flag flapping in the background. The colonel had very serviceable offices in a white plastered building with pink trim and curving balustrades, a former school taken over for a headquarters. Behind it, lined up neatly, were glistening white tents along with rows of shiny white vehicles. When we got there, we found him eager to talk, happy to encounter somebody from outside, even somebody from back home. And he seemed to feel that, despite all obstacles, the best result was about to be achieved. "There have been frustrating moments," he acknowledged, "the demobilization has been slow and is behind schedule." But he was optimistic. "Both sides," he said firmly, "have indicated clearly that they don't want to go back to war. Particularly the soldiers, they have no interest in that. Angola remains on the road to peace." When he thought we'd shut off the camera, he turned away. "There," he said, "I don't think I've told any lies."

The next morning, bright and blue as the UN flag itself, we eagerly acted on the colonel's invitation to visit one of the demobilization camps. The pastors, I'm afraid, weren't happy. They wanted another mission trip and when they learned what we wanted to do, they all grumped off. But we were euphoric, this was going to make for very nice footage. We sped off to link up with the convoy of United Nations vehicles, then followed them, radio antennas snapping in the wind, into the countryside like a bunch of roosters in a self-important parade. Our travels, however, took us not in a speedy straight line but, like a snake or conga line, weaving back and forth to avoid the mine craters. Funcho took possession of what was now his accustomed seat, in front across from Dorta, the lens of his Betacam poised to aim out the window. This morning, however, no herd of cows or old woman hacking away at a roadside field was going to distract him.

We entered a long laneway that took us past what had once been a flour-processing factory, now empty and appropriately bombed-out, its roof gone and all the glass in its many windows shattered. This camp was for Unita soldiers and a couple of thousand of them lived here in tents. Along with the tents were a few grass huts. But, despite the fact many of the soldiers had been there a number of months, the place had an air of impermanence as if it could fold up and disappear within half an hour. There was one solid concrete building that predated the camp—its roof had been blown off, rendering it useless. The plaster on its facade had been painted with a slogan, "viva Marx," next to a four-foot-high portrait of the communist theoretician. Somebody had then used the face for target practice, leaving it riddled with bullet holes. A few bicycles lay about along with things like chequerboards, the only sign of how the inmates or residents or whatever their official designation were expected to while away the long hours of their day.

We pulled up short just inside a guard checkpoint, and the UN staff piled out. From the vehicles in front of us emerged the verification observers, three of them including Charles's Zimbabwean friend, a captain from Russia, and a Norwegian major carrying a clipboard. From another vehicle came Angolan government soldiers sporting yellow armbands. In this operation, each side was permitted to keep track of the other, so these were here essentially to verify the verifiers. The Unita soldiers, who had their own officers, lined up in loose formation. I was surprised to see how well-uniformed they were, all of them turned out in camouflage fatigues crisply starched and pressed, and wearing either berets or neat field caps. This was in stark contrast to the population of the countryside, who were in comparative rags. It was a casual parade, many of the soldiers kept talking and joking even as the UN officers strode along in front of them, doing their count.

I watched. I wanted to come to some determination about these soldiers. They were decidedly young with fresh, boyish faces. None was older than late twenties, many still just teenagers. I looked at them, all jovial with their mates despite being restricted to living for months in this field of weeds, and tried to think where they might be going when all this was over, what they might think or expect or hope their future would hold. Some reports said dishearteningly that they expected only to join "an enormous army of the unemployed." I knew that was the overwhelming possibility. Then

I tried to think about where they had come from. A study amassed by the Southern African Research and Documentation Centre (David Sogge)[1] identified Angolan soldiers as 54% under the age of twenty-five and 40% with less than four years' schooling. This revealed a little, but not much. Were I to take any individual at random, however, what would the last week, month, year, decade of his life have been like? I wanted to make a picture of it, yet found it was almost impossible. What could I know of these lives? What could I know of soldiers or fighters in any situation, for that matter, let alone this one? My personal experience had been woefully limited. I'd been sent off as a cadet in high school to a summer camp where we all marched about in short pants and learned to clean a rifle. But while we'd fired off rounds at targets, there wasn't the remotest notion we'd ever be called upon to kill any real people. It was different here. The war in Angola had been one of raids, ambushes, looting, sabotage, and, of course, landmine planting. The death toll was estimated at 900,000. These young men doubtless had roles in all of it. But what did that mean? The evidence of what they'd done was all about, we'd seen and heard about it for the past two weeks. What I really wanted to know had to do with 'why'.

I thought about the kind of young men back home everybody would want to be wary of, a little too much testosterone, especially when they were in a group, late at night, fortified by a bit of drink. Give them weapons and licence and then watch out. Is that the sort of young men these now-demobilized fighters were? Louts you'd want to keep your daughters away from? Or were they nice boys, the apple of their mother's eye, filled with fears instead of the hopes and plans they deserved at this stage of their lives, taken away from home too early and put into the hands of unscrupulous bosses? Most likely they were a mix of both, but what was their motivation? What moved them, not so much as a group but as individual young men, to sign up, put on a uniform, take up the weapon, and engage in not only the fighting but the continued rampant destruction of their own country and their fellow citizens? Was this motivation political, were they true partisans, committed to their cause? Or were they boxed by circumstances into following orders with no recourse? Was it possibly what they had to do in order to simply survive themselves, the only action going, a substitute for the job and career one might have in a different society? Or was it perhaps something more visceral: they were alive, a good many of their comrades were dead; a large part of their country was wrecked, huge numbers of their fellow citizens were maimed or dead, their own families had suffered god knows what, and this now became life? Simple as that. They were far too young to have a personal memory of the beginnings of the conflict, which meant, in some sense, that they were but cogs in the ongoing wheel. In the histories of war, armies are presented as something amorphous, tools of commanders and strategists and politics. They move against one another according to the immutable laws of battle, the results of their encounters dictated by strategies and physics. However, in the literature of wars, from Tolstoy to Norman Mailer or Joseph Heller, we know armies as something else. They are made up of humans. And when you take the human factor into account, all kinds of things are possible. Humans can be the wild card, their personal feelings running potentially in complete counterpoint to the official version or the official plan. I'd been told that in the past five months, 12,637 troops from the government side, unpaid and far from home, had gone AWOL. They were gone and nobody could find them. Many had doubtless disappeared into the endless slums and shantytowns we'd seen in Luanda. There were no statistics for Unita. I looked at the faces of the young men in their crisp shirts, fatigue pants, and field caps, and tried to believe what everybody from the pastor to the UN colonel had been saying, that this was going to be the end of the cycle. Was that truly going to be the case? All I could tell for sure was that the thousand or so young men in front of me appeared to be bored out of their tree.

There had been so much plaintive hope, so much wishful thinking among the analyses offered to us as we had gone about the country meeting people these couple of weeks, one had to hope at least some of it came true. In a world that was even halfway just, so much longing could not go unrewarded. In one of our interviews, a church official, occupying a pathetically impoverished office, had said to our camera: "We can never have lasting peace without democracy. We must have peace in diversity. We have to learn how to live in diversity, recognize people with other views, other ways of thinking. We need to learn to live with several political ideas."

Two days later, back in Luanda, we went to see the special representative of the UN secretary general who had been sent to oversee the election. Miss Anstee was one of those handsome, middle-aged women who show up on British sitcoms like *To the Manor Born*. She agreed to our interview's taking place out of doors and emerged into the bright sunshine outside the prefabricated building that served as her operations office looking like she'd just stepped aside from a garden party in Surrey. Her auburn hair was swept up into a helmet and frozen with spray. Her blue dress, with its upturned starchy collar, billowed stiffly in the limited breeze. She sported loopy hoop earrings and, at her throat, three strands of oversized pearls. She explained how the UN wasn't exactly running these elections but was going to oversee them and "provide technical assistance to the national authorities working in this process." Her main job was to make sure the international community at the end of the day could say "this is a process that has been carried out by the fairest means possible." I raised the matter of there being thirty political parties competing on the ballot with the two biggest having been involved in a shooting war for a generation. She didn't bat an eye: "If I wasn't optimistic this could be pulled off, I wouldn't have accepted the assignment," she stated. "Although I have been here only a short time, I have been very much struck by the determination of the two main sides to carry through this election. They want to set this country on an even keel. Everybody is tired of war. They want to get on with the development of this country." Then she went on to the fact that seemed so obvious to all us outsiders: "This is a country with enormous development potential."

We wished her well, packed up, and drove a little way off. Then we set up again in a quiet spot under a large tree. I walked around, getting myself ready to take a position facing Funcho's camera. Charles held out his microphone, Lee stood off to the side. I took a deep breath and started to speak the little script I'd written that morning just after breakfast. "What Angola really needs out of all this," I could hear myself intoning, "is a government that will be able to walk the tricky line of representing the population broadly enough to avoid a new outbreak of civil strife." I was one of those correspondents you always see on TV, attempting to gravely sum it all up. "Running a country that desperately needs rebuilding, gaining international credibility and investment but avoiding being recolonized in the process. Not an easy task."

By August, back in Toronto, I had completed compiling our film and had written and published a couple of magazine articles. On September 29 and 30, 1992, the elections were held in Angola. It took several days to count the ballots, at which point I learned that the results gave 49.6% of the vote to MPLA president José Eduardo dos Santos, and 40.1% to the opposition National Union for the Total Independence of Angola, Unita. The absence of a clear majority necessitated, by the prior agreement, a runoff election. It never happened. Almost immediately, the Unita leader, Jonas Savimbi, the boyhood schoolmate of Pastor Julio, announced his rejection of the results of the election. The soldiers in the demobilization camps went into the bush and rediscovered their weapons. By December, 100,000 Angolans were newly dead. I was never able to find out whether Senor Balthasar, the young vice-governor, was among them.

4

OTHER PEOPLE'S COUNTRIES

ANGOLA HAD BEDEVILLED US. What we thought we knew, we didn't actually know at all. But by the time I understood how little I understood, it was too late. I had parroted the assurances of every UN official, soldier, and foreign aid worker that some kind of lasting peace was at hand when it wasn't at hand in the least. The work of my crew had allowed me to return to North America with stirring pictures and succinct interviews, yet somewhere along the way we had missed something crucial. But then, so had almost everyone else—the UN hands, the foreign aid people, the soldiers, the diplomats. The Angola civil war had a life of its own and was destined, any signal to the contrary notwithstanding, to play itself out until in the end it collapsed only and finally with the killing of one of the principals, Pastor Julio's friend Savimbi.

All we outsiders had been no more than, what, hopeful tourists?

This was a difficult proposition to come to terms with, the only upside being the lesson to be wary of outsider predispositions and prejudices as well as dependence on other outsiders for one's thesis. However, there was something else that seemed to me equally unsettling. If we had predicted how badly things would turn out, would anything thereby have been changed? Regrettably, I doubt it. Nobody was going to step in to stop that dreadful disaster; nobody had the will nor did they really know how. Our observations or even our alarmist pleas would have been only that, alarmist pleas and observations. This is the frustration suffered frequently by the outsider in Africa: even should there be cogency, it inevitably flirts with impotence. I think about this whenever I listen to the most widely broadcast voices of our day: the acerbic travel writer, the crusader for more urgent strategies against AIDS, the frustrated interventionist lamenting that nothing was done to stop Rwanda and then Darfur. Everything that comes to us both provokes and simultaneously frustrates us. Bad news evokes a reaction that, for the most part, is automatic: somebody, we say (by this we mean somebody from the outside), must *do* something. Yet, hand in hand with the urgent need to intervene, we are similarly paralyzed. Our words and pronouncements gallop fast ahead while our actions remain hesitant or stymied.

We from the outside world are in some sense perpetually paralyzed by Africa. But in the spirit of reciprocity, we then return the favour. We place Africa into a kind of box where only certain outcomes are deemed possible. All news out of Africa, Paul Theroux wrote, is bad. But it is not simply that it is bad, it is that it comes through a certain kind of filter that then leads irrevocably to only a certain kind of conclusion. On the morning I am writing this, in the autumn of 2006, there is another story in the *New York Times,* another update of the story that has been popping up every few days for the last several years about what is widely referred to as one of the most deadly ongoing conflicts on the planet, that in eastern Congo between government troops, rebels, and invaders supported by neighbouring governments, with fleeing villagers endlessly caught in the crossfire. More senior Congolese officials charging that Rwandan president Paul Kagame has made good on his threat to invade, more charges about Rwandan troops crossing into eastern Congo and clashing with militias there. More United Nations officials saying they are investigating the invasion claims.

On television, meanwhile, a charity is carrying out a fundraiser. The bait is starving children, black children in some country that must have been identified but could be any of a number of countries. There is the standard dusty red-earth landscape, a drought, the hovering prospect of cholera or malaria, malnutrition. The video children, seated on the ground in front of the earthen walls of crude huts, drain powdered milk from plastic cups provided by the charity while their mothers, weary with vacant, distant eyes, wait just off-centre. There are no African men present in this scene. Everyone's clothing is ragged, and flies are stuck to the mucous of the children's nostrils. A concerned-looking white person steps before the camera to make the requisite request for money: "Even a dollar per day will achieve miracles," he tells us as telephone numbers and a Web site address appear. The women and children remain silent, none of them speak.

These two items identify a problem. Or, more specifically, they are symptoms of the problem. Though intended for wholly different purposes, both of them work to exactly the same end, which is to perpetuate an image of Africa as victim, Africa as helpless, Africa as chaos. There is, of course, more than a kernel of truth here, nobody will dispute that there are malnourished children with malaria or AIDS. Or orphaned by AIDS. Just as there are stretches of landscape parched by drought, wars and corruption and atrocities. Which is the problem with stereotypes, they reflect truth on some level even at the very same moment as they are untrue.

But the stereotype sets up something even more disturbing: the notion that Africa—helpless, passive, chaotic—is a child. We outsiders, from the most charitable do-gooder to the most rapacious colonialist plunderer, from the multinational oil company looking for a surefire gusher to the erstwhile rock star turned into a campaigner for foreign aid, have infantilized an entire continent. And, like a child, it can only be managed, looked after, done to. Africa responds in one sense by playing into this. We were puzzled when it was reported some time ago during the installation of South African President Thabo Mbeki that Robert Mugabe, the president of Zimbabwe so properly reviled by much of the outside world, had been given an ovation by the continent's ruling elite gathered in Pretoria. Why had this leader, whom so many right thinkers believed they should treat as a pariah, received such homage? However, it all becomes clear if one accepts the theory that the response had to be because of his having stood up and thumbed his nose at Britain and Europe and America. His infantilized sisters and brothers recognized that Mugabe had taken the next step, he had become the rebellious teenager.

Adjacent implications, however, are deeply disturbing. In 2004, Wangari Maathai, a professor of veterinary medicine at a Kenyan university, was awarded the Nobel Peace Prize for her work organizing small collectives of rural women to plant trees and reforest the country. Many people in Europe and North America were astonished; every report stated how "unexpected" the choice had been. But what was it that was unexpected? That a somewhat obscure African professor should receive this prize? The moment, by any measure, was amazing, the recognition of small steps by someone working very locally to address both environmental urgency and grassroots (and female) power. But the astonishment at both the Green Belt movement's success and the recognizing of one of its leaders may have betrayed a different and highly problematic attitude. It went something like this: how could something so good, so effective as the Green Belt movement come out of the heads of people so passive and helpless as we had come to believe Africans to be? Could it possibly happen without some North American or European NGO organizing or paying for it? Bono, the rock star, at the very least, must have been behind it.

Two phenomena of the late twentieth and early twenty-first centuries discussed in media studies are the "CNN Effect," and the "Pornography of Poverty." Both should be looked at with particular attention to Africa, and both apply to this discussion. The CNN Effect is not restricted to the twenty-four-hour cable news channel, but refers to the effect all media have through a combination of instantaneous but at the same time often superficial delivery of news, especially catastrophes. The foreign policies of faraway governments—and even the UN—are influenced by the fact that the public are moved, and then politicians are provoked into action. But the point is not always of the best sort or for the best reasons. The United States's disastrous adventures in Somalia, 1992–93, are said to be a classic result of the CNN Effect. Horrible pictures of Somali chaos brought to the public through the media made the intervention irresistible, while equally horrible pictures when the intervention went wrong provided huge pressures back home for the Americans to get out. The Pornography of Poverty refers to the use of dismal pictures to pry loose both pity and funds. The pornography comes not so much from the fact that donations are made to charities, but from the voyeurism that is inherent in looking at the images. In an armchair at a great and safe distance, viewers crave, and purveyors deliver, pictures that are ever more dismal, leading to the effect, according to Nigerian editor Rotimi Sankore, of deepening prejudices and making them intractable.[1]

There is nothing new in the desultory view of Africa posted by the outsider. Mary Louise Pratt cites the opinions of Frenchman Michel Adanson in *Histoire naturelle du Senegal* (1757). He introduces "a country overspread with misery, whose landscape consists of burning deserts, rivers and torrents, populated by tigers, wild boars, crocodiles, serpents, and other savage beasts. The inhabitants, Negroes and Moors alike, are described as 'poor and indolent though friendly and docile'."[2] Not enough, unfortunately, has changed. Despite being a multi-faceted, highly variegated continent comprised of more than fifty countries, hundreds of tribes, several language groups, and a variety of religions, Africa far too often is reduced to a single dimension, that of child. This child is either innocent and helpless and available for the rest of us to save, or wayward and driving us, like exasperated parents, to our wits' end. Each characterization is both deeply unfortunate and highly problematic. The problem is that once you get into the habit of such a take, it is difficult to break; all assumptions, all discussions work only inside that paradigm and the paradigm can never be escaped. On the other hand, the unfortunate aspect is that, because of both the stereotype and the paradigm, Africa and African people remain unequal with the rest of the world in that most basic of ways: what we believe they can do. We look at them and decide that we cannot expect much. Objectively, of course, we know that this is not the case, there are competent, visionary people everywhere. But as my journeys took me to other countries and into the bosoms of other projects and ventures, I was repeatedly confronted by what became a common subtext: the pervasive power of the micromanagement of the (usually white) outsider.

— ◉ —

NAIROBI,
KENYA
1997

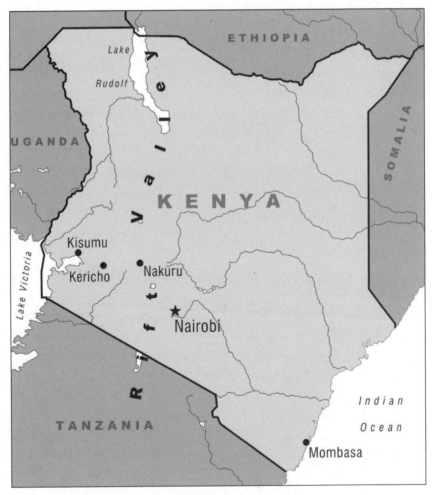

Kenya

5

LOOKING FOR A PROSTITUTE

ON A BRIGHT MORNING IN DECEMBER 1996, I made my way along a breeze-filled corridor in the University of Nairobi medical school, a rabbit's warren of offices—many of them in need of a good paint job—opening off open-air hallways and staircases. I was looking for Dr Elizabeth Ngugi, who had promised to put me in touch with a prostitute. Many prostitutes, actually. I had come to Nairobi to scout locations and interviews for a film, this time about the research that Canadian, and to a lesser degree American and British, scientists were doing in a shanty-town with a group of sex workers who, despite the fact that they had sex several times a day with truck drivers, never became infected with HIV. This extraordinary discovery both puzzled and enthralled the scientific world and provoked people like me to want to find out more about the story. Dr Ngugi, the director of community health for Kenya, had been the main contact between the women and the scientists for almost ten years. She was going to be my connection too.

I found her at her desk, barely visible behind a chaotic stack of files and papers. To say I was apprehensive would have been an understatement; Dr Ngugi was highly respected but I had been warned that she could be acerbic or even unpredictable and nobody wanted to get on her wrong side. A small woman with sharp edges, she stood up and removed her glasses. An automobile accident had put out one of her eyes and disfigured her face, but the fearsome thing was something below the surface. She had the personality of a coiled spring.

Yes, she said, she had already arranged for me to meet the chairperson of the prostitutes' committee. I would find this person in one of the slums, a place called Mathare. The good doctor herself was far too busy to accompany me but her assistant, a friendly-looking woman named Linette who had just breezed into the room, would go with me. While she had us in her office, though, Dr Ngugi was going to provide a lecture. She moved around to the side of her desk. "When people say 'prostitute,'" she said with the ring of a warning, "they only see a woman, not the man. The prostitute, however, is not simply the person who *sells* sex, but also the person who *buys* the sex." Her point was that if there was any stigma, it should be spread around. She was a champion of the women and determined to protect them from having to carry all the burdens by themselves. Here, of course, they weren't prostitutes, anyway. They had been given the far more dignified title of "commercial sex workers." And the very fact they were organized and had a chairperson was in no small measure due to Dr Ngugi's influence.

Eventually Linette and I were let go and soon were making our way through the city in the doctor's chugging yellow Isuzu van. Nairobi was built as a junction on the railway from the Indian Ocean coast at Mombasa to Kampala in Uganda. What ultimately became the Kenyan capital city is at about the halfway point, a good day's trip from both other cities. It is on high ground, almost two kilometres above sea level, which gives it a moderated climate and no malarial mosquitoes. Driving through Nairobi made me happy. By that time I'd already been twice to Kenya as well as Zimbabwe, Angola, and a tiny corner of Zambia. In the same manner it has with other travellers, Africa was getting hold of me; there were moments back home on some wintry days when I would close my eyes and daydream a landscape of acacia trees or conjure the recollection of a precise moment of being seated at a breakfast table with a certain whiff of breeze entering through an open window. It didn't matter that these trips I made usually involved looking at people's troubles; an attraction that was entirely senti-mental and romantic had taken hold. Riding in the subway or walking on the street in Toronto, or when I would be in some other city like London, I might overhear a fragment of conversation in just the right accent, which would be enough to send me into roils of happy sadness, itchy to find the means to buy another ticket. I could now only embrace as good fortune the fact that I had a chance to stay in Kenya for a couple of months and have it paid for by the National Film Board of Canada.

Like all African cities, Nairobi has become horrifically overcrowded, the pleasant colonial suburbs increasingly overwhelmed by burgeoning shantytowns, one of which we were heading toward this morning. When we got there, we certainly knew it; entering the slum was like hitting a wall. Immediately a press of people, carts, and bicycles reduced our progress to a snail's pace. Linette, grasping the steering wheel with tense knuckles, pushed resolutely ahead while I couldn't help but notice that whenever we reached a particularly tight spot where I might think there was no more possibility, magically in front of us, like the Red Sea, the crowd would part. Linette looked over at me. "Everybody recognizes Dr Ngugi's car," she said. Eventually, however, even that wasn't enough and we truly could drive no further. We abandoned the car and set off on foot under the broiler of the late morning sun. We entered immediately into a maze of path-ways, narrow and well-beaten, snaking amongst mud-sided huts. The huts were completely makeshift but at the same time quite tidy, in the way I realized you have to be when your existence is precarious in the face of rain and wind and sun. Some had tin roofs, others were covered by sheets of plywood; a few were put together from nothing more than the cardboard from packing crates. Everywhere was the mania of life, human and more: women scrubbing laundry in open tubs, men braising ears of maize on smoky little charcoal fires, children, dogs, cats, chickens, even a lonesome scrawny goat. Incessant noise assaulted the ears and an overpow-ering smell hit the nose, the kind of infusing stench that sticks inside your nostrils, your hair, and your clothes so that you worry you might never get rid of it. This was produced in the main by steaming mounds of uncollected garbage. Regularly, we had to take giant steps across gutters that ran with stinky water.

We turned a corner at the mud plaster hut of the chairperson for the sex workers' committee. Linette rapped briskly on the door and then, not waiting for an answer, pushed through. "Hello," she sang out. The hut was a tiny two-room affair and, in the second room where I could see the corner of a big bed beyond a half-open curtain, the chairperson of the prostitutes' committee was just completing some business. A startled-looking middle-aged man scrambled to do up his trousers. I was embarrassed, though nobody else seemed to be. "I see you've got company," Linette said cheerily. The chair of the sex workers' committee was a large woman with a round pumpkin of a face topped by a Brillo pad of fluffy hair. She sat upright, a robe half covering her silk slip. Then, when Linette disappeared behind the curtain for a conference, the client, a man with a broad, guileless face, didn't hurry away as one might have expected but took a seat in the kitchen, where he and I eyeballed one another awkwardly.

I couldn't help thinking how unlike a brothel this place was, not to mention that the absolute last thing I'd have wanted to consider was having sex. But then it wasn't my taste in eroticism that was going to prevail. The tradition of prostitution in these shantytowns, I'd been told, went back some eighty years to the days of the railroad construction and was more akin, in fact, to a landlady and her tenants. In the early days, prostitutes were true landlords, the only people to own their own huts. The customers were transient workers away from home needing and wanting, more than anything, their laundry done, meals, a bed in which to sleep. The provision of sex came merely as part of a full-service boarding house. Now, however, it appeared it was just sex.

Eventually the fellow across from me seemed happy enough to talk. He told me his name was Benson and when I asked what he did for a living, he answered proudly, "I am a church worker." Then, as sort of an afterthought, "an Anglican." He was not, it turned out, a proper cleric but a sort of verger in charge of looking after a church building downtown.

The walls of the room were painted a well-scuffed blue. A couple of tattered AIDS posters served as decoration. The only thing shiny and new was an economy-size jar of Vaseline. The lion's share of space was taken up by a gigantic box, almost as big as a refrigerator, prominently labelled USAID—100 gross of condoms meant to be distributed around the neighbourhood to the various other women. Through the flapping shutter of the window, I could see children hopping back and forth across puddles of sewage.

The chair of the prostitutes' committee emerged from the other room, dressed now in a sleeveless shift, and was introduced to me by Linette. *"Muzuri,"* I said. I'd learned a few Swahili terms and figured this would be the time to use them. The woman looked a bit bemused. She was quite large and with Linette, me, and Benson, the room was pretty much filled. Still, the outside door pushed open and two more people squeezed in, a small child and a woman, another sex worker. *"Muzuri,"* I said again. This time everybody started to snicker.

Linette looked at me. "Forgive us," she said, "but we have to correct you." Confused, I wondered what I had done. Linette went on, patiently. "In Swahili there are two parts to the greeting, *habari* and *muzuri,"* she said, "which are the equivalent in English of the question 'how are you?' and then the answer, 'I am fine'." I realized instantly what I'd been doing. "You are turning it around," she continued, "without waiting to be asked, you are greeting people by saying 'I am fine, I am fine'." Everybody had a good laugh at the visiting white man's expense and Benson, finally enjoying some male camaraderie in a room crowded with women, chucked me on the shoulder.

Abruptly, however, the mood then shifted. "Tell Larry about your work," Linette instructed. "He wants to know about commercial sex workers." The two sex worker women looked at one another and then, in the complaining manner in which a factory labourer might deplore everything from the boss to paltry wages, launched into a kind of lengthy discursion. Here, wages or prices were decidedly paltry, 50 to 200 Kenyan shillings per encounter, about one to five dollars, and the work was indisputably tedious and repetitive. The women meandered around these laments for a bit before getting to the core of the matter both for them and for me: AIDS, and the issue of their sisters becoming ill with it, dying, and leaving their children as orphans with no one but the other prostitutes to look after them. This was a great burden. "What are you going to do?" the newly arrived sex worker asked, moving with urgency right into my face. "What is the West going to do?"

Another half hour passed, at which point Linette got up and commenced slapping hands in farewell; she and I were going to leave. Benson waited behind, a hopeful look pasted on his broad face. Out in the street, the main traffic remained children who swarmed us. "Hey, *Muzungu,*" they chirped in their little voices (meaning 'white man'), "how are you?" The only English phrase they knew.

The film we were slated to make was going to feature a microbiologist from Winnipeg, Manitoba, Canada. Francis Plummer had told me some time earlier that he had chosen Nairobi as the place to carry out his work because of what he described as "Sutton's Law." Willie Sutton, he explained, was a notorious holdup man who, when asked why he robbed banks, responded famously, "Because that's where the money is." "So when I wanted to study sexually transmitted diseases," said Plummer, "I came to east Africa." AIDS had not been his focus. In 1984, when he first arrived as a graduate student, it was barely a shadow on the horizon. He had wanted to look at other dastardly infections: chlamydia, chancroid, gonorrhea, syphilis. That Kenya became, shortly, the epicentre for HIV/AIDS was, in a perverse way, a bonus, the sort of serendipity only a research scientist could interpret as that. He got money, opened a clinic and a lab, and now he and his wife, Karla, spent most of each year there with their three daughters, all of whom had been born in Kenya.

Plummer and his family lived in a sprawling Mediterranean-style house on an estate at the edge of a coffee plantation. There was a pool, and a cook, housekeeper, driver, gardeners, and night guards. Their daughters went to the private International School, and for summer holidays the family flew back to Canada. The old colonialism was dead but, in a kind of ironic twist, foreign aid programs in underdeveloped countries had fallen neatly into its place. All the roles of the old system had been refilled. The fanciest vehicles zooming around town belonged to development workers; local authorities deferred to their agendas; the projects offered the best jobs the locals could hope to get. And research scientists were at the apex of this world. To extend the metaphor further, they could likewise be said to fill the positions occupied in the old system by missionaries. The parallels are uncanny. The scientists arrive from far away, carrying a kind of mysterious knowledge that seems indispensable both as it is delivered and as it is received. Around them they gather congregants, those desperate for what they bring or, more precisely, desperate for some form of hope. When they set up shop, a kind of co-dependency develops; before you know it, the locals are providing both the willing audience and the supporting staff. An entire enterprise falls into place. For Plummer's project, collaborating scientists from North America and Europe flew in like visiting bishops if they were high-ups, or apprentice clergy if they were lower on the status ladder, staying for a few days, a week, or a month. Rooms for the rotation of visitors were kept available in the best hotels or in a couple of flats near the hospital and medical school. In the clinic and labs the Kenyan employees—drivers, nurses, technicians—filled the roles communicants and lay preachers would have in the missionary world. Every so often, a select few got sent off for further study to Winnipeg, Toronto, Seattle, or even Oxford, from where they would return to take up positions well along in the local hierarchy.

I was invited over for dinner and Kini'njui, Plummer's driver, picked me up in the doctor's big, white, four-wheel-drive Nissan Pathfinder. We exited the scramble of downtown Nairobi and then zoomed into the winding tree-lined streets of the suburbs. Immediately, the quality of the roads improved. It was just before Christmas and Kini'njui, an intense fellow with a forehead as clear as the open sky, said he could hardly wait to go home to his village, about three hours away, where his wife and two children stayed. There, he told me, they would celebrate by killing a cow and a goat for a feast and then would walk around the village, singing Christmas songs. He had always been a driver, which meant that he had to find work far away from his family and he missed them. But it was an interesting life, he had worked for a while for the wildlife service and had even driven Richard Leakey, the one-time wildlife service chief and son of the famous paleontologists. Kini'njui, moreover, was not lacking in further ambitions: "Sometime," he pronounced solemnly, "if it is in God's plan, I want to visit North America."

When we arrived at the house, it was already almost dark. Plummer, a great burly man—though in a soft kind of way—with curly greying hair and a beard, led me through his gardens. The house seemed to be half out of doors—one of the pleasures of life in a semi-tropical climate— a series of terraces and patios interspersed between different rooms and different wings. Karla, Plummer's wife, caught up to us by the time we got to the living room and showed off the collection of art they'd been putting together, local, most of it, African paintings and carvings solid and carefully selected. Two other guests for dinner waited comfortably in the lounge, an American architect who had designed a new building for the research project's lab, and her husband, a teacher. The five of us sat down. Outside, the black night was soft rather than gloomy; at moments when the conversation ebbed, I could hear crickets from the coffee plantation and doves from the garden. Great pots of rice and savoury chicken stew appeared, as did ample quantities of wine. After we'd consumed quite a bit of the wine, a friendly debate broke out between the two men, Plummer and the teacher, as to which they might label the "queen of the sciences." The notion of a hierarchy would probably have seemed absurd to both men had they been completely sober, but now they were going to have a go at it. I myself was feeling on that tilt between mellow and woozy. The American teacher, sort of a mechanical purist, argued for physics; Plummer disputed this, saying no, it had to be biology. "The urge for sex," he posited, "explains all."

When dinner ended, Kini'njui appeared to take me back to the hotel. When we left, we passed the night guard, his dog, the wrought-iron gate, and the electrified fence, then took off back into the dark roads and streets of middle-of-the-night Nairobi.

The Plummers, certainly to my way of thinking, had an enviable life. They had their house and one staff of people set to do their bidding there and another at the doctor's lab and office downtown. The doctor received a Canadian university professor's salary with all expenses in Kenya looked after; meanwhile, he was undertaking work he found intensely interesting and that looked to be making a difference. He enjoyed the status of a diplomat in the local community while, internationally, especially among scientists working on AIDS, he was a star celebrity. When he needed a break from Nairobi, he could arrange a trip to a conference anywhere in the world. He seemed highly sensitive to local needs. The locals paid him the highest of compliments: referring to the fact that he didn't fuss, didn't push too hard, they described him as "a real Kenyan kind of guy." Kini'njui called him 'the best white man' he had ever worked for.

Whenever I would see him, he seemed entirely relaxed. Yet, I soon realized this was deceptive. Despite looking as if he had just come from lounging by the pool, Frank Plummer had probably been up all night at his computer. He managed to cloak his intensity inside a calm exterior. His work was framed inside a philosophy. He took great pains to explain that he could undertake his research only if he knew there was a kind of exchange that was broadly evident. His primary interest was the shantytown prostitutes, but he had to make sure the clinic he set up in the slum where they lived, Pumwani-Majengo, not only gathered information for his research but delivered medicine and health care to the women and their children. Over ten years, there had been 1800 patients registered at the clinic, of whom 400 had died. But to each, Plummer's team had offered care. As well as malaria, gastrointestinal illnesses, and whatever else the women or their children had, all sexual diseases were treated. "We don't just say, 'you've got HIV, sorry we can't help you'," he said. "We buy a lot of drugs."

"It is ethically wrong to study something and not intervene," he went on. Which was an important discussion to get into because the assertion seemed, on the face of it, to contradict one of the tenets of pure scientific research. The most important discovery Plummer and his collaborating researchers had made was that among the women was a small group who appeared immune to HIV. Their purpose now had become to find out why this was the case. Both in scientific terms and in simple social terms, they were faced with an extraordinary opportunity. In the most optimistic scenario, they believed they might try to mimic whatever it was that protected these women and from that develop a vaccine to protect all the women or even all Africans. But from the standpoint of pure science, their research interest surely would have been best served if these subjects lived lives of high risk, as much sex as possible with as many partners as possible, unprotected. The virus, then, would be there—or not—and he could observe its behaviour. But Plummer had determined he couldn't do that. The clinic gave out condoms and urged the women to use them; he supported Elizabeth Ngugi's efforts at public education and urged his funders to provide her with money to keep giving seminars on how to use condoms. Yet, his research did go on. What made progress possible was the human fact that the women and their sex partners very often failed to take the advice offered. There was enough unprotected sex and enough infection going on that research could proceed. But through it all, the doctor's energies and attention remained divided: he had to be a doctor as well as a researcher. "In Canada or America or Britain," he explained, more than a hint of regret in his voice, "the health care system is there to help people, which leaves scientists free to do their research. But in Kenya the health care system can't provide."

The lab Plummer worked out of and the offices for people like Dr Ngugi, as well as the medical school for the University of Nairobi, were enclosed inside Kenyatta National Hospital, a huge, rambling complex that looked, on a bad day, as if it might fall apart, or at the very least that it ought to be condemned by some passing inspector. Every morning I would leave my hotel to walk to it, passing another hospital first, Nairobi Hospital. This one wasn't very big and had a nice red-tile roof and pleasant landscaping. If you had enough money to pay for them, private physicians and nurses, imported medicines, and ample personal care were reputedly available. You could check yourself in and be looked after in the most up-to-date manner. Another kilometre past Nairobi Hospital, Kenyatta National Hospital was of an entirely different order, a sprawling public institution that somehow encapsulated everything that was—or wasn't—integral to, right with, and wrong with the health care system and Kenya itself. It was surrounded by a congested chaos: taxis and buses roared through traffic circles and along the four-lane road in front of it, scattering and occasionally hitting the pedestrians who, in their hordes, kicked up the red dust on the adjacent pathways from which the concrete of sidewalks had long disappeared. Coming at it from the south, one had to pass the city morgue, an ominous-looking, flat-roofed building conveniently located just beyond the hospital fence. Its smell, in hot weather, was so bad nobody, including the mob of people perpetually congregated in front of it, could last long without covering their noses. From the other direction, from the north, your passage would take you through a zone of taxi stands and then a parking lot in which a cacophonous marketplace thrived, rows of tables with sellers hawking an endless assortment of empty bottles. The pharmacies within the hospital dispensed medicines, but people had to provide their own containers. For this reason, trade in recycled bottles of all shapes, sizes, and colours flourished. On the other side of the parking lot, in a large, empty space, sweltered a gigantic pile of garbage. Old furniture and other junk mostly, but also paper and rotting food both from the hospital and also dumped by neighbourhood residents and businesses. Presiding over this sea of garbage, both guarding and processing it, was a coterie of marabou storks, six or eight of them at any time, brutal birds about one and a half metres tall, untidy, slobbering, with black feathered back and wings, and ugly, bald, red heads.

The grey concrete monolith of the hospital stretched across many city acres. One of the Canadians, who had been there numerous times before, offered to take me on a tour. Ian Maclean had no kind of pass or official permission and didn't seem to need any, he and I simply started walking, making our way wherever we liked down dank halls, peeking at will into rooms and offices. There were lots of people: nurses, doctors, students, clinicians, aides, cleaners, and sick people in beds in the wards, as well as mobs newly arrived and patiently waiting for somebody to have a look at them. What struck me most, though, was the quantity of equipment that seemed to be broken down and utterly beyond use. I had never seen so many discarded desks, chairs, and beds, as well as more important things. In a dusty corner, half under some stairs, lay a complicated-looking item, an MRI machine. It had been donated, Ian informed me, by the government of China. "But there was no contract for servicing," he said, "and when it broke down, that was it."

In-between buildings and wings, we could step out from the shadows into the hot African sun and take a breather in random clumps of weeds and grass and on patches of tired, trampled red earth. Ian marched onward to the buildings of the medical school, where we entered the research wing and labs out of Victorian England. We stopped in to see Mr M in the parasitology lab. Blinking behind too-big glasses and squeezed into a too-tight lab coat, he proudly held up a jar labelled "1958." Inside, preserved in formaldehyde, was something about the size and colour of a softball, which turned out to be the foetus of a baboon. I tried to figure out why he was hanging on to stuff like this. Mr M selected another from among the jars on his shelf, this one containing a black leech, which he was pleased as punch to show us, explaining how "such a simple thing caused the death of a four-year-old girl." When did that happen? I asked. "In 1984."

At last we made it to the hospital coffee shop, which consisted of a couple of tables and a window through which you could buy a Coke or a Fanta orange. Already seated at one of the tables, in complete jeans-and-open-neck-shirt uniform, was another of Plummer's associates, a Scot from Glasgow named Denis Jackson. Ian and I joined him and ordered a soda. In short order the conversation got round to AIDS and, remembering the conversation from a few days earlier with the prostitutes in the shantytown, I pushed Jackson for his perspective. He simply shook his head. "It's going to become, if it hasn't already," he said, "a tropical disease." I looked at him. Western observers going to Africa to look at AIDS are always like visitors to a train wreck, we see how awful it is, how completely horrible, but we want to believe it can be cleaned up. And when we describe things, we try to keep that in mind, searching always for some notion of hope. But here was a radically different take that confirmed the kind of directionless frustration I had already encountered in the women. After several years of trying to find ways to make progress on the disease, including stints in Somalia and Congo, Jackson seemed resigned. Not defeated, and, in fact, quite angry. But nonetheless resigned. By "tropical disease," he meant something the rest of the world would get used to watching Africa endure. Back in North America, AIDS had been quarantined into a disease primarily of gay men and addicts who used needles; rates of infection had slowed dramatically. At that moment, early versions of the drug cocktail therapies that would soon manage the disease were starting to become available. In Africa, none of this was happening. Earlier that morning I had taken a look at the obituary pages in *The Nation*, the Kenyan newspaper: photograph after photograph of youngish-looking men and women all with funerals announced. "Do you think," Jackson posited, "that if malaria were killing thousands of people in America and Europe, we wouldn't have found a cure?" I thought about the prostitutes and the shantytown orphans. That was the big gap between my country and here. In North America, AIDS had been an emergency that now seemed to be coming 'under control'. That very fact might spell Africa's doom. In Africa, it would always be an emergency. But, like all the other emergencies, that just made it one more fact of life.

6

HAWA

*T*HE COMMERCIAL SEX WORKER who was going to work with us for our film was Hawa Chelangat. She was thirty-seven years old, had five children, and lived in the requisite mud hut at the far end of the shantytown called Pumwani-Majengo near the community water tap and also the community garbage heap. The selection decision hadn't been mine to make. At the World AIDS meeting in Berlin the previous summer, Doctor Plummer had made a presentation about immune sex workers, what in the AIDS science world they were now calling "persistent sero-negatives," and everybody from French TV to the BBC and PBS had responded by sending documentary and news crews. By now, film and television crews were not unusual in the shantytown—everybody wanted a prostitute as part of their footage—so pressure on the sex workers, especially those who were negative to HIV, was intense. To deal with this new demand and to spread the work around, the women had developed a system. With each request, they had a lottery to choose who the next star would be, no one being permitted more than one performance before everybody had a chance. It wasn't really that they expected to be stars, there was not a television to be found in the electricity-deprived slum; what participating with the outside visitors really meant was money. We agreed to pay a designated sum through the clinic to whoever was chosen to work with us, the amount calculated to make sure it covered whatever would be lost in trade. We expected to keep Hawa busy for about ten or twelve days so that amount of lost business should be compensated. On top of the fee, we promised a couple of hundred extra dollars as a contribution toward school fees for her children. The gig, therefore, was both a break from the regular routine and, we hoped, more than attractive economically.

At our first meeting, Hawa didn't fit my preconceptions of a shanty-town prostitute. The other women I'd seen, either at Plummer's Pumwani clinic or during my visit a month earlier at the house of the chairperson of the committee, had the aura of a hard life about them. Some were roly-poly, slightly overweight; others were brassy, tarted up with lipstick, eye shadow, tinted hair, costume jewellery. Hawa, by contrast, was tiny, with perfect, smooth skin. Not that there was much skin to see, she was a Muslim. When she entered the room when we first met, it was in a rustle of long flowing robes and hijab or head scarf. She walked with a pronounced limp, the result of a childhood bout of polio, and spoke and understood only rudimentary English. Joann Ambani, a nurse from the clinic, told us she would have to be present at all times to translate. But Hawa's natural intelligence was evident, and once we got going, it was obvious she had an unerring instinct for the camera, so much so that she could easily have been given a position in Actors Equity.

By this time I had a crew. I had brought three people with me from Canada: Charles Lavack, a cameraman; Terry Woolf, a sound technician; and Bonnie Dickie, a general assistant. This was the first trip to Africa for each of them. In Nairobi we hired two locals, Steve Kamau and Henry Kungu. Steve, a gregarious fellow of about forty, had worked in the small but busy film-support business in Nairobi and knew both camera and sound well enough to assist Lavack perfectly. He spoke Swahili, so could provide translation when we needed it and, an entrepreneurial type, had a new van for hire so could provide us with transportation. In any tight spot, we expected Steve to be our general 'fixer'. Henry, the driver who came along with him, was so quiet it took a while to realize that he was also observant to the degree of missing absolutely nothing, something that would turn out to be invaluable. As well, I hired Rachel Taylor, the wife of one of the foreign researchers based in Nairobi, to be our manager, to handle the daily finances and help us set things up.

It was natural to want to make the shantytown central to our program. Though chaotic and difficult, that place was the most visually vivid of any scene in Nairobi, so on the very first day of shooting, off we went. At least on a rudimentary level, I understood the objectives of the scientific research as well as what an overwhelming problem HIV/AIDS represented for Kenya; indeed, for all of Africa. But it's possible for such things to remain abstract. The shantytown dramatized everything that was going on in a way nothing else could. To be there and in the clinic in which Plummer's project operated was to be at the very epicentre of the day-to-day pitch of the contest; this was the front line of the battle with the war going on all around.

We decided to follow the daily routine not of high-flying outside scientists, but of ordinary Kenyan nurses and clinicians, the people who staffed the clinic. Every morning from the parking lot of the University of Nairobi medical school at Kenyatta Hospital, a driver named Daniel, a bow-legged, shiny-faced man nicknamed "Mr D," loaded a white van with a supply of vials and cooler boxes. Then into the front seat beside Daniel slid Jane Kemene, one of the longest-serving nurses at the clinic, while into the empty seats in the back piled four, five, or six women, all with their white lab coats under their arms. It was like a morning going-to-work scene you'd find anywhere in the world; the women joked about events of the night before and gossiped about their children. In a cooler next to his feet, separate from the coolers with medical supplies, Mr D had several litres of fresh milk from a cow he tethered behind his house at the edge of Nairobi. The shantytown provided a ready market for this milk and Daniel's profitable side venture.

Nairobi in the early morning had the same frenzied push of any large city, the only difference perhaps being that as well as the vehicular traffic, hordes of people were on foot, kicking up dust on the red earth pathways that snaked everywhere sidewalks might have or should have been. The vast array of older vehicles with badly tuned engines produced a persistent haze of black fumes. The noise of everything, the traffic and the people, was cacophonous. Amidst the jam of traffic lumbered a few large buses, though public transit seemed to be provided mainly by garishly decorated vans, which were everywhere, especially dominating the curb lanes, where they crowded out all other traffic. Designed for twelve passengers, these vans, called *matatus*, were habitually overloaded with fifteen or twenty people, inevitably including some who were forced to cling to the outside, shirt-tails flapping in the wind. A good number of them were owned, we'd been told, by ministers in the government and ran unhindered by regulation, volume compensating for low price and their touts grabbing the fares.

We climbed into Steve and Henry's vehicle to follow Mr D, and entered into downtown, a passable facsimile of a modern city with the requisite high-rise office buildings and swooping, porticoed hotels. We passed the US embassy (which, within the year, would be bombed by Al-Qaeda) and the Aga Khan's Ismaili Muslim mosque. The jam of traffic and also the hordes of people on foot never let up, everybody in Nairobi seemed to be out on the street, nobody could be left at home. Though Henry pushed hard to keep up, a couple of times we lost sight of Mr D, once when a truck loaded with garbage changed lanes and set itself between us. For almost a city block we were showered with the refuse spilling and blowing out of the back of the garbage truck, thankfully most of it paper. For my crew everything was new and exotic, so much so that Lavack found it impossible to resist rolling videotape, either through the side window of the van or, at stop lights, standing up with his torso pushed through the sunroof, which could be slid open. A French Canadian from Manitoba with a ponytail, granny glasses, and a long, flowing, black beard, Lavack brought with him an irrepressible enthusiasm. Terry, fiddling with his recorder, popped up beside him with his microphone and boom pole to get sound. Terry made his home in Canada's Northwest Territories, in Yellowknife, and responded to our new exotica by reminiscing endlessly about his sled dogs back home. "Be careful up there," Steve warned just before Terry yelped. Two young men running by the side of the street had made a grab for his watch. Down they sat and all the doors clicked locked. The watch remained, dangling from Terry's arm, still intact though its band had been ripped. Steve looked stern. The episode was our warning and put to rest any doubts about hiring security to accompany us in the shantytown.

By this time we'd reached the city's central market and the assembly area where country buses and dilapidated for-hire Peugeots left for points north: Nakuru, Naivasha, and the northern Rift Valley. We made a sharp turn and were confronted abruptly by the shantytown—a mass of tin-roofed huts as far as the eye could see, stretching through the valley of a desperately polluted urban stream. Henry slowed down, as Mr D in front of us also had to do. I rolled my passenger window down but Steve said rather that it should be rolled up. Again, he pressed the button to lock all the doors. The street noise, which was already extreme, became even more intense. Crowding in from the periphery, to turn the road into a barely passable single lane, were hawkers and merchants of every sort. Their wares included fruit and vegetables, soft drinks and water, but mostly clothes. Instantly I understood where the used clothing North Americans and Europeans give to charities ends up. Those bundles deposited in church basements become not charity for some poor naked misfortunate, but product to be resold a half dozen times before landing with a final customer like the boy I spotted sporting a bright red Harvard sweatshirt or another with a T-shirt advertising Jim's Sunoco, Kitchener Canada. Alongside the clothing were shoe merchants, who appeared to be doing particularly well with great heaps of their footware loaded onto tarpaulins stretched out on the beaten ground. Behind them, half out in the open or sometimes under awnings, were support industries: people vigorously applying polish to the about-to-be-marketed shoes and rows of tailors pedalling on treadle sewing machines, making adjustments and repairs to the clothing, as well as men with steam irons applying a last-minute press to a pair of trousers or an elaborate lace tablecloth. To supply it all were lorries, slowed to a virtual crawl, or, just as often, the product was brought in by human carriers, men like draught animals pulling heavily loaded hand carts or carrying the stupendous loads right on their backs.

For five minutes, we bumped along at a crawl. Through the back window of the van in front of us, I could see the heads of the clinic workers bouncing radically as Daniel negotiated each canyon-like pothole. What would this place be like in the rainy season? I wondered. At last, parting the crowd of people, Daniel turned into a narrow lane and through a gate. The clinic was a whitewashed building set off in its own protected compound behind a high fence. The noise from the surrounding streets remained intense but at least there was physical space. We parked next to the project van, and got out into the already hot morning sunshine. Jane, Joann, and Njagi, the doctor, had disappeared inside, donned their white coats, and were ready to start processing patients. As we followed in and commenced our set-up, Njagi, a precise young man wearing tinted glasses, seemed bemused by the presence of yet another film crew. Jane, by contrast, stylish with a ribald sense of humour that she found hard to bottle up, took it in stride; she'd already made friends with Lavack and was having a swell time posing flirtatiously for the camera.

Abruptly, though, she broke with this jolly mood and beckoned me to a tiny office. "Sit down," she said, pushing a chair toward me, "I need to show you something." From the drawer of a desk, she pulled out a large book, black with red binding. It had the look of an accounts ledger, which, in fact, it was, of sorts. "Death Register," it was labelled. Nurse Jane opened it, drawing my attention to the neat columns in ballpoint pen ink: one after the other, names, places of origin, ages, dates of death of all the women who'd been part of the clinic program since it had begun, but who had died of AIDS. More than 400 of them.

The waiting room for the clinic was a cramped lean-to furnished with rows of wooden benches. Tacked to the walls were signs in Swahili forbidding spitting and posters urging condom use, cartoon characters telling you how your next boyfriend could bring you the unwanted gift of an early death. A dozen women, some of them with small children, already occupied the benches. Their numbers rapidly increased as more came in. Once summoned inside, each would sit down with one of the clinicians first to get her records updated. Then she would slip off her shoes to get weighed and have her blood pressure taken. Finally she moved on for medical attention, the main focus of which seemed to be the taking of a number of vials of blood. We and our film project were an inevitable disturbance but,

I sensed, also a bit of entertainment. Watching white men in short pants setting up thousands of dollars' worth of equipment for an end product none of these women expected ever to see was yet another absurdity that fit in well with the many other absurdities life offered. One of the women referred to Lavack with his bushy beard as "Moses" and soon that word got around and everybody started to enjoy it. As for me, I kept a watchful eye out for Hawa. At last, through the throng outside the gate, I could see her coming, a tiny figure in long, colourful robes.

Hawa had been part of the project from the beginning. Plummer told me he had first encountered her in 1986, more than ten years earlier. Since then, at least once a week, she had made her appearance in order to keep her end of the bargain with the researchers and the project. Once in the clinic, she went through the same sequence of procedures as the women ahead of her, except it was all done with Lavack's camera in her face and Terry's microphone and boom pole hovering. Dr Njagi straightened the collar on his white jacket and nurse Joann stepped closer in to be ready to provide translation. It all took a while. Though it was a hot day, Hawa was in layers of clothing: beneath her robe she had a dark blue sweatshirt, under that a T-shirt. Finally she was able to stick out a bare arm, into which Njagi poked the first of several needles. As the vials of blood filled, Joann affixed a label to each: Patient number 935. "Because she is sero-negative," she explained, "we need more from her. We watch her even more closely than the others." Everyone was careful not to make too many assumptions, but had, at any time, her tests come back positive instead of negative, it would have been devastating, and not just to her personally.

Each vial of blood from each of the women—including Hawa—was plugged with a colour-coded top, red, purple, green, yellow, to designate its destination once back downtown in the lab. All samples would first be tested for HIV, a test called Elisa. From there they would then enter a vast system of research corridors to break them down into every conceivable component part. The blood would be peered at under microscopes, spun in centrifuges, frozen in liquid nitrogen, and transported thousands of kilometres by air to Toronto and Winnipeg. The cells would be sequenced and cloned, all in the hope of yielding information not just about the person from whom it had been taken, but more global information about the immune system of the human race and the diabolical virus that was attacking it. As the morning wore on, the crowd in the waiting room grew. The sheer numbers of people waiting in queue made it seem like the process at the clinic might never end, yet, miraculously, shortly after noon, everybody had been attended to. The staff tidied up, locked the doors, and, carrying their coolers filled with the morning's collected specimen, piled back into Daniel's van for the return trip to the university and the labs.

We, however, had decided to stay on. As Mr D's van disappeared toward the highway, we, on foot, turned in the other direction. To the aroused interest of the locals, our entourage of foreigners, dressed like safari tourists with video equipment, boom poles, backpacks, and notebooks, departed the clinic compound now in the wake of a small, limping woman wrapped in blue robes and a hijab. Because she was going to continue to translate for Hawa, Joann Ambani remained with us. On top of that, we'd been persuaded to hire security. Joann assured us she knew somebody and brought around Randall, a huge man, black as coal, well muscled, and dressed, despite the heat, in a dark, tight-fitting suit and tie. Randall looked like a handler for Evander Holyfield, the heavyweight champ, and carried with him an ebony cane, the sizable bulb of which he kept whacking purposefully into his open hand. Nobody was going to mess with him.

In the world of urban settlement, a shantytown, whether in Rio or Calcutta or Nairobi, is a unique form of social organization. "Organization" is perhaps not the right word because it does not in fact seem to be organized at all. A shantytown is the antithesis of organization and urban planning, foreign to imposed order. Rather than official, it is an "unofficial" place, laying claim to territory that exists on the edge; there are no official addresses, no official census or count, and that is the way it seems destined to stay. It is where people squat, sometimes literally, when they have no alternative, when the world and all of life have overwhelmed them and cast them aside. It is not a place where control or planned progress of any useful sort is very often possible. Poverty, of course, is the defining characteristic, poverty of the most grinding, burdensome, wearying variety. All around is 'make do'; use what you can; squeeze in; do it any way possible;

ask no questions. And, inevitably, such poverty exacts a toll. The worst of its impacts is that a shantytown becomes a place that defies hope, certainly the kind of hope that makes people cast an eye on the future and say, "A better day is coming. Therefore, let's build a school for our kids, let's make a park in our neighbourhood." A shantytown isn't a place that has anywhere within its genetic code the probability of ever becoming much improved over its present grim state, mostly because its citizens are not likely to be in a position to invest in its improvement and, if they are, they are not likely to do so. Just as an inmate has no interest in the collective future of his prison, shantytown dwellers are unlikely to have an interest in the shantytown's future. The tendency is to be consumed completely by the personal; the tendency is to want out. If your fortunes take a turn for the better, you do not work to make better your shanty and your shantytown; you leave it. That is the governing rule.

Yet there is another side to it. Any place where people live is a community. In the same manner as the suburban estate or the rural village, a shantytown is where lives get lived. Joy is found and sorrow endured. When I was in the shantytown, I wanted to look at it with these things in mind. I wanted to absorb it all in some manner that might help me make sense, not sense in the standard, objective way—that is, to dismiss it as a place where people didn't have enough, period—but to see it for what it must be if this was all you've got; if the last thing you could afford in the midst of your poverty was to let your surroundings depress (or oppress) you. For a woman like Hawa and her children, this was the stage, the platform upon which and out of which they lived their lives. It was neither abnormal nor super-normal, for there is no 'normal' to compare it against. There are just series of realities and this was one of them.

Our film objective was to follow Hawa on a journey that, for her, was a daily routine, the walk from the door of the clinic to her hut. The distance was about a kilometre, but the journey was going to cover not only the entire geographic distance of the Pumwani shantytown, but its social trajectory as well. We'd discussed how, along the way, she might do certain things, and on cue she did everything we requested. At a vege-table stand, she stopped to examine a carrot, then purchased a dozen small potatoes. A little further along, she fingered some fabric but decided not to buy. Then, things we hadn't imagined to schedule started to happen. People stopped to chat. At each encounter, high-fives were exchanged as a standard greeting. Hawa's face would break into a luminous grin and her head would cock to hear gossip or news exchanged in rapid-fire Swahili. A bicycle with three sacks of charcoal strapped to its back fender rattled past, almost dumping the unsuspecting Lavack bent over his camera and causing Hawa to step hastily out of the way. A group of men, lounging outside the community latrine, gave her (and us) the eyeball, whispering among themselves. In return, Randall issued them a particularly stern stare and whacked his ebony cane once more against the palm of his free hand. We continued along the crowded and well-beaten path, Hawa carrying her small sack of potatoes and passing and greeting her friends, her neighbours, her customers. It occurred to me that what the shantytown was, in fact, was not just a community imposed on an overburdened landscape in defiance of what centralized authority might have wished, but an eminently natural, organic environment, more natural, in fact, than any place with imposed order. Like a patch of weeds blooming at the edge of a well-tended field, it was the most organic of human communities and potentially, like the weeds, hardier than the neighbouring field crop and likely to outlast it.

Hawa Chelangat had arrived in Nairobi about fifteen years earlier from a town in the far western corner of Kenya. Her motivation for coming to the big city, she ultimately told us, turned out to be the same vague impulse that sends millions of people the world over from the countryside into cities: hope offering the fantasy of a different, more interesting, and more profitable life. The same motivation even I, half a world and a vast culture away, responded to when I was eighteen and moved myself to Toronto. Yet, as is the case everywhere else and in everyone's life, once the move has been made, a version of real life that has not been anticipated—and is quite distant from any fantasy—sets in. Hawa had a husband for a while, but he left. She moved in with an uncle who had a place in the shantytown. She'd had two children already by that time and was at a loss as to how to support them.

When we finally made it all the way to her hut, I was anxious to see how we might film it. Our audience in their comfortable bungalows or apartments back in North America would need to believe that whatever they saw was a place where a family lived. What we found when we got there wasn't so much a free-standing structure as a rabbit's warren of passage-ways and enclosures, Hawa's and her neighbours' all glommed together. It reminded me more than anything of the forts I remembered creating with my friends in the corner of the schoolyard in late autumn when we stuffed all the fallen leaves from the maple and oak trees into rudimentary frameworks to make tunnels where we could hide. Hawa's place, however, wasn't some play fort but a residence she had to share with her children. Eventually we reached a couple of rooms, one of which possessed a small window that looked out into daylight and through which the tinny noise of somebody's transistor radio came in. Along the walls were two low-slung, futon-style couches, mattresses only, and, in the middle of the space, a small table covered delicately by a neat, white, lacy doily. Only Bonnie, Joann, and I could fit with Hawa into the small room. Lavack and Terry had to set up with their camera sticking in through the window. Steve went to see if he could get somebody to turn off the radio.

When her husband had disappeared, Hawa faced a serious problem: she had no money. With Joann translating, she told us what happened next. A 'friend' offered to help financially in exchange for sex. It seemed like a solution. "Except I soon found that one friend was not enough," she said. More children came into the picture and she could no longer stay with the uncle. In order to get a hut of her own for what were eventually five children, she needed even more money. While telling us this, she looked at the floor. "It was hard at first," she recounted. "Being with more than one man was not easy for me because I had only been with one man." But she decided to be philosophical: "Soon I realized that this was a good business, and I got used to it because I had no alternative." The men ultimately multiplied into a systematic routine of four or five each day. They came to visit her at the hut when the children were off at school. Since her children were older now—her oldest son, Swele, was eighteen, Misha was sixteen—surely they would know about her line of work. What did they think? we asked. How did they react? Hawa's response to this line of questioning was to stonewall. "The children don't ask when Mom has a visitor," she said.

"in our culture it is not the business of children to know too much what adults do."

No sooner had she said this when the children started to arrive home. It was now late afternoon. Swele and Hussein showed up first, then little Juma, who was seven. They attended different schools, all outside the shantytown. We broke up our interview configuration and set up in the open passageways outside Hawa's hut. The daughters weren't there yet, which provoked Hawa into a round of anxious enquiring as to their whereabouts. She disappeared back into a dark corner of the hut to prepare supper. Swele and Hussein took their books and settled themselves on the packed earth floor of one of the passageways. The boys were well dressed, almost preppy. Swele wore a pink v-necked sweater and an open shirt and creased trousers. The younger Hussein was curious. In short order, he jumped up and began asking questions about the video equipment. He was intrigued as any young boy might be and wanted to examine everything, touch it and look through it and listen to it. Terry placed the headset over his ears and fiddled with the recorder so he could listen to the sounds that came in through the microphone. Lavack let him view the pictures on our tiny monitor, hand-held and wireless, that showed what was being seen through the camera lens. But while Hussein was excited and engaging, Swele remained aloof, which caused me to wonder about him. Was he sensitive? Angry? Smart, for sure. But what was his life really like? What went on inside his head? What on earth would be his future? Against a mud wall of the hut, he sat by himself with his nose in his books. When Hawa came out with a plate of sliced bread and a tray of cups filled with milk, he put a pointed question to her. It wasn't until months later, when we got a translator to listen carefully to all the Swahili conversation exchanged between Hawa and her children, that the nature of Swele's question was revealed: "When," he asked, "are they going to leave?"

Eventually we did wrap up, said a round of good-byes, and set off back to the clinic, where Henry had stayed with the van. It was a long trudge. The day was waning, but the boil of the shantytown society still maintained some energy. About halfway along, just past the community toilet where the unemployed men hung out, we encountered a scuffle. There was some fierce shouting and then two young men sprinted off, whizzing past us, chased by four others. Randall stepped round like a mother hen, steering us away from the altercation.

The next morning I came out from breakfast to find Henry in the van reading the *Nation*, Kenya's newspaper. On the front page were blurry photographs depicting some kind of incident, a violent scuffle, by the looks of it. I looked over Henry's shoulder at the paper. "It was a lynching," he said. Though apparently the whole town was talking about the story, Henry seemed matter-of-fact. "It happens all the time," he said, "robbing and purse snatching and pickpockets are a very bad problem, so this is how they solve it. Somebody gets set upon by a thief, they yell, a crowd gathers, the crowd chases the thief, and if they catch him soon he is quite dead." What made this a story of more note—other than the fact that somehow a photographer for the *Nation* happened to be present at the crucial moment—seemed to me to be the extreme violence of the event. A pickpocket operating on one of the *matatus*, the crowded ones at rush hour, had snatched a woman's purse—much in the manner Terry had almost lost his watch the morning before. The pickpocket had then leaped from the bus and run off. But in this case, it had not been the first incident, he was known, and had been working a number of the *matatus*. At the end of the day, a group of drivers set off en masse to hunt him down. Apparently they knew exactly where to find him and when they did, they dragged him off to a vacant lot, where they 'necklaced' him. It was apparent from the pictures what this meant but I asked Henry anyway, just to make sure I understood completely. I was not wrong. The unfortunate fellow had been trussed up, then a tire was placed around his neck, its well filled with petrol, and set alight.

Where did this take place? I asked Henry. "On the edge of the Pumwani shantytown," he said, looking at me carefully. "Right by where we were yesterday."

7

SEARCHING FOR HAWA'S SECRET

HERE'S NOTHING," FRANK PLUMMER TOLD ME one afternoon, "quite like the rush you get when you discover something new. It's better than any drug you could ever imagine." This was a few months after our first meeting and we were sitting in the small office he kept in his house by the coffee plantation. He was animated to the point of agitation, his eyes shining with unsuppressed excitement. What he had discovered, by that summer, was the beginning of that intricate chain of commonality among his cadre of sex workers. It had become a given over several years of keeping tabs on Hawa and the other women who remained free of HIV, a number that hovered around sixty out of the clinic's total population of patients, that no matter how persistent or repeated their exposure to the HI virus, they were not getting infected. Other women were becoming sick and dying. Even the customers of these women were disappearing, presumably also getting sick and dying. Yet they themselves remained healthy; when their samples were submitted for the Elisa test, the little tubes didn't come back clouded with yellow.

Science, the methodical verifying of answers to questions that get posed as hypotheses, happens these days through two things: a gathering of data through the endless taking of samples and reducing them to cogent bits of information, and then a similarly endless poring over that information. Thanks to technologies such as computers, an infinite number of things that could not be done previously are now possible. Material that would have taken lifetimes to sort and calculate previously can now be tabulated in seconds. But what is still required is the human mind to make the choice decision, to say, let's go down *this* pathway rather than some other one, let us ask *this* question among all possible questions. Plummer had all kinds of numbers and statistics garnered from the blood work done with the sex workers. His technicians, day after day after day, peered down their microscopes, entering whatever information they found into the computer stream. Then, usually at night, Plummer would sit in the dark of his home study, the glow of the computer screen the only light, worrying over the results, trying to trace patterns, looking for anomalies. His eureka moment one night was the realization that he should focus his questing attention not on the women who were sick but on those, like Hawa, who remained well. If they could figure out for certain what was keeping these women out of harm's way, they might be on to something huge. In short order, he came to the conclusion that the information he had was good enough for him to suspect an actual immunity, a natural immunity that was peculiar to the women who remained well. His next thought was this: was it possible to extract that and bottle it and thereby protect everybody?

His thoughts turned to the legendary stories about how Edward Jenner, the country doctor in Berkeley, had stumbled upon the milkmaids who didn't fall ill with smallpox when one of the frequent epidemics raged through eighteenth-century England. It occurred to Jenner that because of their job, the young women had been exposed to cowpox and that was the factor that made them resistant to the much worse disease. That discovery provided one of the first insights into the human immune system and permitted a vaccine to be developed to protect from smallpox. How had Jenner felt, Plummer caught himself wondering, when he had come to that understanding? How long had it taken to realize the full ramification of his finding? The continent of Africa was overrun with theories about HIV/AIDS, some of them voodoo-like and bizarre. That very week I'd read in *The Nation* separate reports that the disease was not a virus, that it was a Western plot, and that it could be cured by honey. Likewise, the continent had been taken over by a growing plethora of bona fide AIDS researchers looking at everything from the nature of the disease to the nature of its spread to the potential for vaccines. On top of that, an increasing number of researchers were looking into social and economic impacts. Among all these, Plummer and his associates knew their project was only one brick in the vast wall. But because of the information that had come to them and its surprising nature, they had been able to turn a dramatic corner.

By this time, Plummer had a small army of colleagues, underlings, and associates. These included not only researchers from Winnipeg, Canada, and Nairobi, Kenya, but also from Seattle in the United States and Oxford in Great Britain. Helping organize the vast material, the chief number cruncher was a rumpled statistician from Holland, Niko Nagelkirche. Plummer considered him brilliant. Then there were young scientists who had first encountered the project as students and for whom, without any doubt, trips to Africa were coveted perks. One of these was Kelly MacDonald, who would later head up a vaccine project at Toronto's Mount Sinai Hospital. MacDonald had first come under Plummer's tutelage as a graduate student and unabashedly loved her episodes in the field. While happy to work in the lab back in Canada, she found that forays into the front-line clinics helped her both gain and keep perspective, giving grounding to the theoretical and making everything not abstract but real, not to mention more poignant. "This is easy on a theoretical basis, when you're looking at molecules," she observed one afternoon after a session in the clinic. "But when you encounter people directly and see their faces, when they're laughing and joking with you, when you give them the pills for their pneumonia and understand that the six kids sitting outside are all their children, then it's harder." She paused for a moment, her eyes misting over, then went on: "Sometimes I retreat behind the science because otherwise it's just too overwhelming. I really like these people." Time in the field had helped the young researcher understand something else about her profession. "You can't cure all these people," she said, "so you go back to your lab and do the research because maybe that's the way you can do some good."

It was one thing to come to the conclusion that a certain number of sex workers in a foetid Nairobi slum might be immune to HIV. But the critical question, in fact the only useful question, remained: why? What did Hawa and the others in the small group of women have that nobody else had? What was protecting them? This, then, became the task for the scientists, to set up a whole new set of questions and hypotheses to help them travel usefully through that quest, searching, isolating, paring things down, testing. By 1998, and the time we were making our film, Plummer's researchers had identified at least one commonality among the resistant women: they all shared similar HLA. Human leukocyte antigens, for the uninitiated, are cell markers that everybody possesses. But the significant thing is that not everybody has the same ones, nor do we have them in the same combinations; there is a variety of types and they come in a variety of combinations. As the HLA taken from the white blood cells in the serum samples of the sex workers was typed in the lab and the information put into the computer, what had become apparent was that the resistant women had, first, rare types of HLA, and, second, that the combinations of HLA molecules in the resistant women took on similar patterns. If one wanted to look for the things that separated these women from all the others, this, the scientists believed, was important. They knew that the job of the HLA molecule, perched on the surface of every human cell, was to function as a sort of traffic light, telling visitors when to proceed or when to stop. When it saw the approach of cells it didn't like, for example, it would summon surveillance cells to destroy them. That, in a nutshell, is how the immune system works. So if the HLA combinations peculiar to the resistant women were what was turning on the red light to halt the entry of the HI virus, then that could be considered pretty important.

The HLA line of pursuit was important for another reason. It meant that the resistant women were being protected by something cellular in nature rather than by something triggered by antibodies. One way the body's immune system works is that when a foreign virus invades, antibodies are created. Most vaccines, in fact, pursue this line of defense; a tiny bit of virus is introduced into the body in order to stimulate the production of antibodies, which will then do their work, like cruising police cars targeting any future arrival of recognizable foreign cells. The smallpox vaccine works like this and it was how the cowpox antibodies were able to fight the smallpox virus in the milkmaids. But HIV is different. No vaccine producer as yet believes they can afford to introduce even the tiniest bit of HI virus into a human body. The virus is too dangerous and too volatile. Once introduced, it could not be controlled and the outcome could not be predicted. However, were one able to depend on the cellular response of HLA, that could all be avoided. A vaccine based on HLA would fight HIV without the dangerous tactic of introducing any of the virus itself into the body.

It fell to MacDonald and a young Oxford PhD student, Rupert Kaul, to pick up the work. "Our job," MacDonald said in attempting to explain the primary part of their research, "is to determine which variants of the HLA specials [the resistant women with the unique combinations] possess. Is there a single mutation in their DNA?" They froze the cells of the resistant women, transported them by air freight to labs in Winnipeg and Toronto, thawed them, and then, in those North American laboratories, allowed them to continue to grow. They watched them carefully. "When we find something that appears brand new," MacDonald said, "we clone and sequence to give us something to experiment with." What their experiments showed was encouraging: the combinations and types of HLA peculiar to the resistant women stimulated the immune response to HIV better than all the others. The stop lights they operated were working.

They considered they were in possession of some extremely interesting information. But it wasn't nearly enough. Each question answered, in fact, often simply leads to the realization that there are two more questions needing to be asked; a road turned down usually merely points to the existence of another fork in the trail and yet more choices to be made. It was like this with the project they were on. They had to determine the next step in the journey. One thing they concluded was that they needed to find out whether the HLA patterning, and the resistance itself, might be genetic. Was it something families shared and, therefore, could it be inherited? To pursue this, they decided to ask Hawa to help them track down some of her relatives.

Hawa came from a region in the western part of Kenya, in the tea country in the direction of Lake Victoria. Her parents were dead, but her extended family all lived back there. The researchers decided to pay a visit to these brothers and sisters and cousins and gather as much information as possible from them. A host of tasks would be part of such a visit: blood samples would have to be taken and brought back to determine the HLA types; everybody would have to be tested for HIV. Frank Plummer held a meeting to plot out a strategy. He himself wasn't going to go to do the research, almost a day's journey from Nairobi just to get there, he was going to deputize some of the Kenyan staff. Dr Njagi was part of the strategy meeting, but the lot to make the trip fell to Joann Ambani, the nurse and our translator. A second meeting was held that included Hawa. A plethora of questions came up. The first one: how to explain the research once they got there? Everybody in Kenya would have heard of HIV/AIDS, but the relatives were country people, it might not be something they would have at the very front of their consciousness. The country cousins would be suspicious both of the disease and of medical scientists. Then there was the process of the gathering of the samples, it was probable that none or few of them had ever had blood taken before and so this itself would raise their suspicion and fear. "You will have to give them something in return," Hawa instructed. It could be anything from gifts for the elders to money, she wasn't specific. Ultimately it was decided that medicine for any possible ailments would be indispensable among the gifts. "There is a lot of malaria," Hawa pointed out. "If you treat that, they will appreciate it." Joann nodded and added malaria medication to her list.

The big question, though, was how to explain the actual motivation for the research. How would they justify to the people they were visiting the intricate information the scientists wanted? Why, the relatives might well want to know, were these people descending on them as opposed to their neighbours or anyone else and looking for AIDS? What was the connection to their sister or cousin Hawa? The critical matter that threw the researchers into a true quandary was that Hawa's relatives didn't know she was a prostitute. It seemed impossible to carry out their study without somehow letting that information out of the bag. But how could they do that, wasn't it beyond what they could possibly consider ethical? It was at this moment that Hawa herself bought decisively and definitively into the research. She was being manipulated and her privacy was being invaded, not just in front of strangers from around the world like us, but also in front of her family. Yet she stood up to the plate. On the matter of the explanation to her family, she spoke firmly. "Leave that to me," she said.

By the time the day came to make the journey, the enterprise had ballooned into a major expedition. At six o'clock in the morning, Kini'njui arrived at the clinic in Plummer's Pathfinder. Joann was already there, waiting with a full quotient of medical supplies, drugs, pills, sample bottles, syringes and needles, the things she would need for her own work plus gifts for the family. A cousin of Hawa's who wanted to tag along on the trip arrived with a suitcase as well as with little Juma, Hawa's youngest son, in tow. While we were helping Kini'njui load everything into the 4x4, we looked up to see Hawa herself emerge from the door of the clinic. Festooned in a billowing yellow dress, not unlike a wedding dress or something Scarlet O'Hara might have worn in *Gone with the Wind*, she sashayed out with no thought whatsoever as to how her voluminous skirt was going to be contained within the crowded vehicle. Her hair was tightly braided and she had thrown aside, for the journey to the country, her Muslim hijab. Instantly we all realized the degree to which this trip was not a chore but an event! With two vans, theirs and then, following, ours with driver Henry, Steve, and my entire film crew, the relatives had better be ready for an inundation.

Our little convoy set off ready to cut, before the end of the day, a great swath through the middle of Kenya. We would be heading north and then west, dipping down from the heights of Nairobi into the Rift Valley and then skirting round that and going towards the lakes and the sunset. At lunchtime we stopped for fuel and something cold to drink at Nakuru. Everyone got out to stretch cramped legs and stand around on the hot pavement of the filling station with our bottles of pop. It was good to be in the country, as if only by doing so could we actually comprehend what a grinding and stifling place Nairobi was. Nakuru, though bustling, was a farm town, in complete contrast to the big city. There were farm tractors on the main street as well as wandering cows munching the boulevard grass and tearing the leaves from low-hanging branches of the shade trees. The air smelled different; one had a sense of the stage of the crops in the fields. The maize looked as if it was going to do pretty well this year.

Soon after Nakuru, the character of the country changed. We entered more undulating landscape, rich, lush, and emerald green. Tea plantations as meticulously manicured as golf courses lay interspersed with forest stands of eucalyptus trees necessary to fire the tea-drying ovens. The plantations, like soft carpets, were exceedingly easy on the eye. The endless fields of tea bushes were laced with pathways in which you could see the bobbing heads of the pickers. All picking had to be done by hand, a careful selection of the top leaves, which were then dropped into sacks worn around the pickers' necks. Signboards along the highway advertised the plantation owners, by and large still big British companies. We were getting close. Kini'njui signalled a turn and we followed down a dirt road that merged off the highway, leading ultimately onto a bumpy trail that dead-ended abruptly at a small farmstead. A herd of seven or eight cows, an overgrazed pasture, a circle of mud brick and plastered huts with corrugated steel roofs: the rural compound of Hawa's uncle and aunt. We stayed for a few minutes inside our car to watch the scene unfold. Hawa, in her extraordinary dress, spilled out of Kini'njui's vehicle right into the arms of her elderly uncle. It was an enthusiastic reunion. Juma was scooped like a kitten into the nest of his extended family. The cousin from the city danced from one foot to the other, pleased as punch to be home.

Except for Hawa, her cousin, and little Juma, we were all going to spend the night in the local town, Kericho. We checked in at the Tea Hotel, a big, lumbering, grey stone place that might have had its best days in the era of Evelyn Waugh. It was dusty and slightly dowdy with not a British colonial in sight, but eminently serviceable and welcome after the long day's drive. After dropping our things in our various rooms, we gathered for a drink, gins and tonic on the terrace. The last to arrive was Joann. I could tell she wasn't completely relaxed, but was fidgeting and distracted. Finally she confessed she didn't know how things were going to go the next morning. She was worried about everything she had to do. She felt a right to be apprehensive, this was a huge responsibility, both to deal properly with all the strangers who were Hawa's country cousins, and then to her boss, Dr Plummer, and the science. What if the relatives resisted? What if she got there to take her samples and no one showed up? At this stage of things, the full burden of all the science fell on her narrow shoulders.

She needn't have been so worried. By the time we returned to the small farmstead of Hawa's uncle the next morning, the sun had climbed and it was getting hot. When we drove into the compound, a broad field complete with cows and goats and chickens, a gathering had already assembled near to the main house with more people arriving by the minute. Right away, among the throng, I spotted Hawa, once again in her billowing yellow Scarlet O'Hara dress. There were perhaps fifty people, all seeking shade under the tin roof canopy of a kind of outdoor enclosure held up by posts just next to the house. Children, old people, lots of people Hawa's age. In the far back of the crowd, I saw Juma being teased, tickled, and pampered by some teenage girls. Lavack and Steve set up our camera and Terry commenced handing out candy we had brought along for the kids who quickly massed around him. The gadgets in the arsenal of the foreigners knew no bounds. Bonnie had a Polaroid camera and immediately became popular by offering to snap people's pictures and doling out the prints. The enterprise took on a festive rather than a solemn air; this was a family carnival, like Christmas or Thanksgiving. Joann, looking visibly relieved, took her various boxes of needles, sample bottles, and all-important medications and headed for the house, whose outside wall, even though it was April, still bore a Christmas decoration, a stencilled poinsettia. She slipped into her white lab coat; a brown rabbit, obviously a pet, hopped past her feet at the open door. The relatives took notice and visibly started to prepare themselves both psychologically and physically for the procedure to come. A ragged queue formed of people ready to go in for their session with Joann. It remained a mystery what explanation Hawa had made to her family, but trust was obviously there.

8

HOW DO YOU DEFINE PROGRESS?

ATE IN 2004, ALMOST EIGHT YEARS after shooting our film, I was back in Nairobi. I found a number in one of my old notebooks, picked up the phone, and dialled it. I left a message at the Pumwani clinic for Jane Kemene, now the senior nurse, and when she called back, I asked about Hawa. "Still alive," Jane answered, "still well, still part of the project and, most important, still negative. You should pay her a visit." The next morning I clambered once again into the back of the old white van, Mr D still behind the wheel, for the ride across town to Pumwani and the clinic. Joann Ambani was now no longer with the project but a number of familiar faces remained; Jane Kemene slid into the seat beside me. Not much had changed, either, for the trip across town, Nairobi streets were as crazy as ever. When we reached the edge of the shantytown, the squeeze between surging humanity and potholed roads slowed us to the snail's-pace crawl Mr D had been enduring for years. The cacophony of hawker noise was deafening. Finally, as we managed to push through the throngs of people, I noted that the clinic too was exactly as it had been, protected from the outside chaos only by its flimsy fence.

Though the study of the sex workers was continuing and the operation of the Pumwani clinic was still under his authority, Frank Plummer and his family had left Kenya by this time and returned to Canada to take on, among other things, a position as head of a large federal government virology laboratory in Winnipeg. Kelly MacDonald and Rupert Kaul were both in Toronto, where they continued to work on AIDS vaccine projects. Kaul, now an assistant professor at the University of Toronto faculty of medicine, was still looking at information from the resistant sex workers; MacDonald was pursuing various other routes, including having developed a prototype vaccine that she'd carried far enough forward to try it out on monkeys. The AIDS vaccine search in general, however, did not report any dramatic good news. It had proven painfully slow going. This was a stubborn puzzle, defiant indeed to being unlocked. The buoyant expectations of half a decade earlier had been reined in sharply. The biggest advance had been engineered by a group from Britain's Oxford University, who, making use of the research done by Plummer, had come up with a vaccine prototype, which they had steered through two phases of human trial. They'd hit a wall, however, on the third part of the trial, the one where after a vaccine has been proven safe, researchers try to determine if it will, in fact, prove effective.

I'd been watching Kenya now for a decade, and had to acknowledge that it was in grim shape. The national HIV infection rate hovered around 10%. Among specific groups, like sex workers, it was possibly as high as 80%. People were dying at a steady and ever increasing rate, leaving their jobs empty and their orphans behind. The middle generation was collapsing in a decimation that left the old and the young huddled under the onerous burden of being one another's caregivers. Foreign outsiders searched through their thesauruses for ever more hyperbolic adjectives to give full linguistic effect to the devastation, human and social. Kenyans themselves seemed to exist in a kind of state of stunned shock. They knew things were bad, but what could they do, other than get up every morning and go to work or to school or out into their fields? AIDS, like malaria, was now part of their reality. As the Scottish doctor, Denis Jackson, had predicted those years earlier when we shared a soft drink at the Kenyatta National Hospital, AIDS had become a tropical disease.

The fight, though, couldn't be given up. One of those people still very much on the scene and prepared to pursue an unblinking confrontation was the woman from the public health department with the plain-spoken manner and the damaged left eye. I called Elizabeth Ngugi, who quickly offered a day to spend with me. When she showed up, Dr Ngugi was not alone. With her was a woman named Bernadette, the current chair of the sex workers' committee. Bernadette smiled crisply. Dressed like a no-nonsense church woman and carrying a voluminous handbag, she was very much into her role as chairperson. I joined the two of them in Dr Ngugi's vehicle and we headed into the middle of the city, ending on a street of commercial stores selling things like electrical appliances and auto parts, all the dusty, unadorned components of construction and service businesses. Dr Ngugi pulled up in front of a whitewashed building with a sagging green awning and a smudged sign: New Aden Hotel. "Come with me," she said and stepped out of her van. The director of community health for Kenya, wrapped in traditional dress, a colourful ground-length print with matching fabric folded around her head, west Africa style, headed for the front door past a beer vendor and a clot of loitering men. It was then that both I and the men noticed what she held in her hand: two pieces of wood, one light blond, possibly pine, the other dark ebony, about eight inches long, shaped and polished to a smooth sheen. Wooden penises. When she saw us looking, she laughed.

Inside, the hallways were gloomy as night. Up we went, three flights, at every landing stopping to exchange enthusiastic greetings with the people who emerged as if on cue from the doorways of the rooms—grinning women, not to mention the odd bamboozled-looking man. Finally, we reached the top, where an open door showed into a small room, the kind of low-end hotel suite that would never be rented by a foreigner. Seated on the sagging bed and two hardback chairs were four women, all of them prostitutes and all of them very large. Dr Ngugi and Bernadette pushed in. Like a practised show host, the doctor leaned forward, flourishing, like a pair of chopsticks, the two penises. From her bag she pulled a fistful of shiny foil packets. "Now," she said in her heavily accented English, "what we are going to undertake is a demonstration with a group of women ("undertek a deemonstration with a grup of weemen …") who work out of this hotel. Just to review what they know about condom use." The largest of the women, a bemused beauty named Alice squeezed into an orange miniskirt, took the light-coloured pine stick and one of the condoms. The ebony rod was grasped by Florence, a crinkly-faced older woman. The sound of tearing could be heard as the foil encasing the condoms was ripped open.

Though nobody could tell me what the statistics were among all Kenyans in general, condom use among prostitutes in Nairobi, I was told, had risen to 75%. Three quarters of sex worker women used condoms three quarters of the time, or some variant of that pattern. This was thanks to relentless public education, posters everywhere including in bars, and one-on-one instruction such as what Dr Ngugi was carrying out that afternoon. It also was a result of an extensive supplying of condoms as part of the foreign aid programs of North American and European nations. Condom supply was part and parcel of almost all aid packages and AIDS strategies. Yet, 75% use among this highest of risk groups seemed hardly good enough. In all the strategies regarding HIV/AIDS, one would have thought simple prevention should be the easiest, the cheapest, the most potentially fruitful. If ever there was a disease that was easier to prevent than to cure, it was AIDS. Yet, in a country with at least a 10% rate of infection, prevention was obviously not working very well.

A major culprit, every woman in Kenya I listened to told me, was the men. "The customers," the sex workers reported, "will pay more for no condom." Despite all the information so chillingly available, men still blindly insisted on taking their chances. And men still liked a lot of sex. Kenyans, I'd long since learned, could not be conveniently boxed into a single, monolithic cultural category, it was much more complicated than that. Tribal customs entered into the mix, as did levels of education and levels of adoption of Western-influenced urbanization and modernity. Everywhere were pockets of conservatives, both traditional and Christian communities. But there was also a much more relaxed and recreational attitude toward sex than exists in general Western culture. In the view of not all but certainly many Kenyans, the right for an African man to have multiple partners might as well have been enshrined in the constitution. One young fellow not yet out of his twenties, who, if education was a measure, couldn't have been unaware of contemporary issues, for he had a university degree and a job with the government, told me bluntly: "A man who makes love to only one woman is not a real man." When I raised the matter of AIDS, he looked at me as if this *muzungu* was truly wearisome. Sighing deeply, he marshalled his argument. "I might die from AIDS, it is true," he said. "But in the time it takes for that to happen, I might also die in a shooting, a traffic accident, a war, or of some other disease." Life was a lottery and he would take his chances.

A second problem was the foreign moralists. The condom strategy, though condoms were readily available, was buffeted by conflict and contradiction. That it was fine to fight AIDS, though apparently not with artificial methods of birth control, was a growing rather than a lessening opinion. The Catholic Church had weighed in from the very beginning to make the condom distribution strategy difficult; the prevention of a deadly disease and the control of a deadly epidemic were at odds with papal encyclicals on reproduction. As time went by, Protestant groups likewise made condom use difficult, though with a different argument: if you handed out condoms, they asked, weren't you condoning and perhaps even encouraging promiscuity? Wouldn't it be better to promote sexual abstinence? From America, the Bush presidency in the middle of its first term had shown up with what, on the face of things, appeared a generously financed HIV strategy for Africa, the President's Emergency Plan for AIDS Relief (PEPAR). But what was good and generous and forward-looking about it was negated by being overlaid with moralistic qualms about condoms. Christian fundamentalist elements pushed hard to keep contraception very low in, if not completely out of, AIDS strategies; what would come down the pike in the final analysis would be something called the ABCs of AIDS prevention, 'A' standing for sexual abstinence, 'B' for being faithful. Condoms only showed up belatedly with 'C'.

In the big picture of AIDS and Africa, varying strategies moved around one another like independent tectonic plates. In an ideal world, they should have been complementary, but regrettably seemed often competitive and exclusionary. On the question of a vaccine, the great volume of public attention had appeared to wither. Too long and expensive a process to ever get one approved, declared some; too many mutations in the HI virus to hope to nail it with a single vaccine, said others. What the most vocal agitators wanted at this moment was that Africa should have what North America and Europe already had: anti-retroviral drug therapies to keep alive all the people already infected with the virus or even ill with the full-blown disease. Finding ways to finance the enormous expense of such an undertaking and overcoming the formidable logistical problems of distribution and administration had taken front place on the stage. The other approaches hadn't worked, and people now wanted to believe that somehow this might. Except for some groups, often with financing from the Christian Right in America, who were trying to promote sexual abstinence, the notion of prevention appeared to have fallen way down on the priority list. Too difficult. Close to impossible. Too discouraging.

Elizabeth Ngugi then escorted me to the second appointment of our afternoon. We headed to a shantytown on the opposite side of the city from Pumwani, proceeding through the usual rigmarole of parking our vehicle, then treading through a push of people and the stench of the litter-filled road toward the hut of the woman Elizabeth wanted us to meet. We turned down a narrow pathway between mud walls, and she eventually pulled back a curtain masking a doorway. Inside, in a hut that was so dark it made its occupant seem almost a troglodyte, was a skinny, near-emaciated creature in bare feet and a rag dress: Jennifer, a sex worker in the late stages of being ill with AIDS. The rainy season was just commencing and all the concerns I had every time I saw the architecture of the shantytowns would soon come to fruition. In the rain the night before, a section of the mud wall outside Jennifer's hut had collapsed in a heap, exposing the crude sticks that served as lathwork. Even inside the hut, the packed mud of the floor stuck to my shoes. Elizabeth and Bernadette squeezed themselves next to Jennifer onto the lumpy, damp pillows on the cot. Outside, a few of the curious gathered round to peer in the doorway. Elizabeth wanted me to meet the children, Jennifer had six, so one of the women from outside was sent scurrying off to round them up.

Elizabeth took a look at Jennifer and attempted to start a conversation, in large part for my benefit. She began to question and then explain the sick woman's symptoms. "She has chills, she has fevers, she has severe headaches," she said. With each description, Jennifer nodded her head weakly and looked ever more miserable. Many were the days when she could do nothing but doze. She had made her living as a prostitute and though it was terrifying to consider how long into her illness she might have continued to work, it was unrealistic to think that she would not have done so. But certainly there was no living to be made now. The miserable end was upon her and her only hope to mitigate anything about it was seated on the bed beside her. "We are here," Dr Ngugi pronounced firmly as if sermonizing to the whole world, "because we have to organize to look after the children. We have to make certain Jennifer gets what she needs." Throughout the shantytowns, as, one by one, women became ill, she and Bernadette were organizing caregiving co-operatives. Jennifer obviously needed a lot. The woman who had gone to fetch her children returned, having rounded up four out of the six. Their bewildered faces appeared in the doorway whilst in-between them pushed a mangy dog.

Against this backdrop, my reunion with Hawa was a pleasure and a relief. She arrived while I waited at the clinic, a familiar figure emerging from the crowd and entering through the gate into the compound. Her limp was still there and she was wrapped in a purple and yellow hijab. She recognized me with a big smile and we slapped hands in greeting. The passage of time had not been unkind. Even though she was eight years older, now forty-five, she retained her smooth skin and girl-like features. She, also, was not alone. Accompanying her, wrapped similarly in colourful cottons, was an attractive young woman. This, she said, was her daughter Asha. I had hardly ever seen Hawa without some combination of her five children, and Asha, whom I remembered as a child of twelve, was now all grown up. Hawa told me she had recently been on a trip to visit her relatives up in the tea country, the very relatives we'd put in our film, and, while there, had contracted malaria. Feverish now, she needed the clinic to supply her with pills to fight it, though she had sufficient energy to giggle merrily when I began to recall the weeks we'd spent working on the film. Our conversation with her limited English and my non-existent Swahili was a bit of a struggle, but Asha translated. I asked about her life. Asha, it turned out, was not only grown up, she had a two-year-old child of her own, making Hawa a grandmother.

Hawa continued to answer questions about her family. Yes, she said, her younger boys were doing fine. They were still in school. What about Swele? At this, she looked at the ground. Apparently not so fine. "He got into some problems," she admitted finally. "And he has gone away." That was as much as I could pry from her and I had to wait until later for Jane to confide that Swele, the promising student who had seemed so fiercely proud when we'd encountered him as a teenager, had become entangled with a ring of thieves operating in the shantytown and now was locked up in Nairobi's prison.

Finally, as every time previous, it was Hawa's turn to go in to see the doctor. I was left free to look out past the big fence into the roil of the shantytown. Hawa was alive and, except for her malaria, she appeared well. But other than her children growing up, not much had changed. Those years earlier, she had talked about quitting prostitution and going into some small business. Her idea had been that she might become one of the middle persons in the used-clothing industry. It seemed, however, she was still a prostitute, working, as ever, out of her hut at the far end of the shantytown. Not long before, in a story that had appeared in newspapers in Canada, one of her fellow HIV-resistant sex workers, a woman named Agnes, complained to a reporter that while the international scientists were "getting rich and famous from the research they were doing on our bodies," she and her sisters were seeing none of it, continuing to toil for a few dollars a day. One might have argued that this accusation was unfair; the international scientists weren't making themselves wealthy, this wasn't some kind of scam. But could you truly convince a woman like Agnes of that—or Hawa, for that matter? They saw only that precious few of the bright hopes we foreigners brought in with us had materialized in anywhere near as dramatic a manner as people had been led to believe they would. Hundreds of thousands of person hours had been invested in work and research, millions of words had been spilled in articles and books and speeches arguing and telling the story, millions of dollars had been expended, and things remained as they had always been. I thought about my own project. We had made our film and people in North America had watched it on television. Students in universities had looked at it as part of their studies. But what had it all meant? All of us foreigners were perpetually flying in, flying out; breezing into people's lives, breezing out. And here was I again, though this time contemplating how everything was still a disaster, if not more of a disaster than ever. At which point, Jane Kemene appeared at the door of the clinic, motioning me to follow her inside. We headed to the small office at the back of the clinic, where Jane sat herself behind the desk, pulled open the top drawer, and removed the same large black book with the red binding I'd taken my first look at years before: the Death Registry, her accounts book. She opened it and, her finger moving down the columns, started counting. Jane still kept it meticulously up to date; since I'd last been to the clinic seven and a half years earlier, 152 new names.

--- ◉ ---

ARUSHA,
TANZANIA
2002

Tanzania

9

PASTOR NTAKIRUTIMANA

*I*N 1998, JOURNALIST PHILIP GOUREVITCH, a frequent writer for the *New Yorker* magazine, published a book: *We Wish to Inform You That Tomorrow We Will Be Killed with Our Families.*[1] The title, certainly among the most chilling ever used for a work of non-fiction, was excerpted from a note Gourevitch obtained from a seventy-year-old Seventh Day Adventist pastor, the Reverend Elizaphan Ntakirutimana, who had fled from his village in the hills of southern Rwanda to Texas, where two of his children lived and where Gourevitch tracked him down. On a tumultuous day in the spring of 1994, the note had been delivered to the pastor from a group of his church colleagues huddled inside the community hospital compound in a village called Mugonero, and he had carried it with him ever since. The colleagues were all Tutsis; Ntakirutimana was a Hutu—tribal names the whole world is now familiar with (though less tribal names in the strict sense as castes within a long-standing feudal-like system). The note, brought early in the morning to Ntakirutimana at his house by the community's sole policeman, was a plea from his colleagues for their lives. Their desperate hope was that he might have the power to save them. That he continued to keep it with him many months later and after his flight from his country half a world away to the United States was a reminder that he had failed. Later in the day in question, his colleagues were all killed, shot or butchered with machetes, along with a couple of hundred other people who cowered behind the walls of the Mugonero hospital compound. The question, however, was whether he had simply failed to save his friends and colleagues, or was there something worse? While Ntakirutimana maintained that he had done what he could, to others, including writer Gourevitch, the note indicated something quite different. He had failed to *try*, and potentially even shared complicity in their deaths and their being marked for death. Within twenty-four hours of Gourevitch's paying his surprise visit in September 1996, Ntakirutimana was scooped up by FBI agents armed with an indictment from Louise Arbour, the Canadian newly instituted as prosecutor for the United Nations war crimes tribunal, the International Criminal Tribunal for Rwanda (ICTR). He fought extradition from the United States, but lost; under chapter seven of the United Nations charter, all countries are obliged to cooperate with indictments emanating from the Security Council. In due course he was transported to a jail outside the Tanzanian town of Arusha, there to join another of his sons, Gerard, who had been a doctor at the Mugonero hospital and had been arrested in Ivory Coast, to which he had fled. The two were each charged with three counts of crimes against humanity and three counts of genocide.

Nobody will ever dispute that in the spring and summer of 1994, in the tiny central African country of Rwanda, unspeakable things happened. Close to 800,000 people (rounded off to a million in some histories) died, one in eight of the country's population, in waves of rampant slaughter so horrible it stretches credulity even to try to imagine them. The killing was universal; it started in the capital of Kigali but took place in every region of the country, in towns and rural villages and off in the bush. It was relentless, day after day, night after night, with those doing it reportedly falling down exhausted, grabbing a few hours of sleep to recuperate, and then recommencing their grisly enterprise. One reporter calculated that for the more than three months it went on from April to July, 8000 people would have had to be killed every day, day after day after day. But the most sobering thing is that it was all so intimate, accomplished not by "smart bombs" or gas chambers or even by rifles, but by machetes, clubs studded with spikes, and garden hoes, the most close-up and physical of means. To actually kill someone with a garden hoe has to be one of the most difficult things anybody could attempt—it demands an engagement that is total, a commitment that is fierce. The blood, sweat, screams, and death struggle of your victim will embrace you, splatter all over you. Even should that person be nowhere near your size, chances are your clothing will become torn, your skin will get bruised and lacerated, and even though you prevail, you will walk away with your heart pounding and your pores streaming. There would be no way to escape or rationalize what you had done. It is not war but murder.

When the slaughter ended, two major questions have plagued the world ever since. What on earth had caused this to happen? And what could or should have been done to prevent or stop it? On the first, there are theories running the full gamut from a carefully orchestrated genocide, complete with centralized planning and direction, at one extreme, to, at the other, a proposition of chaos, ancient animosities run amok in the absence of social order. The "genocide" term the official world has embraced may or may not be useful. It takes the fact that most of the victims were Tutsi and most of the killers Hutu, and notes that inciting factors like Hutu radio broad-casts employing highly charged language—such as calling Tutsis *inyenzi* or "cockroaches"—fanned the flames of ethnic hatred, and from this, it draws its conclusion. The brief history of modern Rwanda supports this analysis. The colonial Belgians divided the ethnic groups and raised Tutsis to be sort of overlords inside the two-tier structure that formalized a terrible culture of abuse of those out of power by those who held it. When colonial times ended and the more numerous Hutus managed to take power, they returned the attitude in full.

Alternative or competing analyses tend to emphasize politics over strict ethnic considerations. These point out, for example, that among the first to die were Hutu officials of moderate bent, like the president of the constitutional court, Joseph Kavaruganda, or the prime minister, Agathe Uwilingiyamana. On the morning of April 7, 1994, Uwilingiyamana, a forty-one-year-old former high school teacher who had young children and whose husband was a university administrator (subsequently killed also), was chased through the grounds of the United Nations Development Program compound to which she had fled from her own residence, and then butchered against the garden wall while Belgian soldiers, who would themselves soon be killed, looked on, impotent. The very first to die, in fact, was the Hutu president himself, Juvénal Habyarimana, whose dictatorship had run for twenty years. His plane was shot out of the sky as it was returning to Kigali from neighbouring Tanzania, where he had been forced into a meeting to agree to power sharing with his political enemies, the Tutsi-dominated Rwandan Patriotic Front (RPF), who, for the past four years, had been invading his country from the north, from bases in Uganda. The genocide theorists argue that this plane crash was a pre-arranged signal to Hutu extremists to start the massacre, but that argument ignores the point that no one (except presumably the perpetrators) yet knows if the heat-seeking ground-to-air missile that brought down the president's plane was fired by Hutus of an extremist political party, by French paratroopers working on their behalf, or by RPF fighters. What you had, no matter which analysis you select, was an invading force, a dead president, established order collapsed.

On the second question of what the rest of the world could or should have done, hindsight has provided us with the luxury of conceiving numerous strategic courses. The objective fact, shamefully undeniable, is that in the immediacy of the events, the outside world did virtually nothing. The United Nations Security Council ordered the small contingent of international "peacekeepers" already on the ground in Kigali, headed by Canadian general Roméo Dallaire, to follow its initial mandate, which was to monitor only, and ignored his pleas for a beefing-up of his support and a freeing of his hand to undertake some kind of action, any action. France and Belgium, who had soldiers in Kigali as well as lengthy histories of enmeshment with the Habyarimana regime, will have to examine their own consciences. These things said, one might neverthe-less wonder what a few outsiders performing as international soldiers could possibly have achieved in terms of stemming such violence as occurred, even were their forces doubled or tripled or quadrupled. And the answers to all such questions are doomed to remain forever in the realm of the speculative.

What also has to be confronted, of course, is the nightmarish socio-logical or psychological question: what exists inside human beings that can cause them to become turned from people who have lived their entire lives peacefully—going about their family and community business, being husbands, fathers, sons, daughters, neighbours—into the active killers so many of them would have had to become in order for this to transpire on such a scale? How did they enter into such madness and sustain their fury over so many frenzied days and weeks? Tribal or ethnic or caste identities, even ancient grudges, aside, what, on a purely human level, could have brought, in the case of Pastor Ntakirutimana, a seventy-year-old man, pastor in a Christian church, father of five grown and educated and accomplished children, a man who had dedicated all the labours of his life to securing his position, and then his second eldest son, not long back from medical training in the United States at St Louis, married with three small children of his own, to this place where they should be hunted halfway across the world and then charged with having committed the most heinous and terrible crimes known to man? The charges stated that they had "partici-pated in an attack on men, women and children who had taken refuge in the Mugonero (hospital) complex," and in ensuing days they had "searched for and attacked Tutsi survivors and others, killing and causing serious bodily or mental harm." What kind of person could become unhinged, if you will, from the proper, sedate, responsible life they, by all accounts, had been living and undertake such deeds as they were accused of? And then what kind of person would remain after it was over?

When I first saw the Ntakirutimanas, *père* and *fils,* it was through a bulletproof glass wall. In the end, what the outside world had done was set up a court. Chastened by the world media and the scale of what they eventually realized had happened in Rwanda, the UN Security Council in 1996 issued a directive to establish the International Criminal Tribunal for Rwanda, its task to put on trial those fingered as instrumental to the Rwanda atrocities. In total, only about seventy people were named, all high-level people—generals, cabinet ministers, bishops, mayors, police officials—among whom the Ntakirutimana son and father, a lowly pastor and country doctor, I couldn't help but think, seemed the least. In the autumn of 2001, seven years after the massacres in their homeland, five years after Gerard's arrest in Ivory Coast and a year after the pastor had been extradited from the United States, their UN-sponsored trial began in Arusha, Tanzania.

On a bright morning in early May 2002, I surrendered my camera and deposited my driver's licence with the security intake desk at the Arusha International Conference Center. "Don't worry," laughed the guard, a jolly man of substantial girth, as he handed me a laminated visitor's badge. "You will get them back." The conference centre had originally been donated to Tanzania by the government of China for use as a regional trade facility for local agricultural products, but now had been commandeered by the United Nations and converted into a courthouse complex. "Complex" is a good word, for it would be hard to describe the sum of the centre using other terminology. A confounding arrangement of sloped walls, corridors, catwalks, strangely shaped rooms in-betwixt surrounding and interconnected courtyards partly landscaped and partly paved over, it left the impression it might have been produced by an architect on Speed.

I started down a dimly lit corridor, negotiating, along the way, two additional security checkpoints. Then I spent twenty minutes trying to follow directions to Trial Chamber Three, there being three courtrooms in the building as well as an enormous number of offices for everybody from judges to prosecutors to police to witness programs to public relations. The whole of the place was made up of three buildings, labelled Kilimanjaro, Serengeti, and Ngorongoro, these connected by walkways, tunnels, and bridges, in any one of which, I realized quickly, it was possible to get hopelessly lost. A guard in shiny, polished boots told me I was in Kilimanjaro when I needed to be in Serengeti. In a stairwell, obviously going in the wrong direction, I encountered an Indian woman who worked for the court. She turned me around, muttering, "This building is sick." Finally, I made it.

On first impression, Trial Chamber Three resembled not so much any sort of courtroom I might have been used to as it did a theatre stage or set for a television program. There must be a standard blueprint for the courtrooms the UN constructs for its trials. I had been to the one in The Hague created inside a former insurance company office building for the accused from former Yugoslavia, and it was exactly the same. The layout ran side to side, rather than front to back. Perhaps ten metres deep, the room was easily four times that in width. At the back, on a raised, blond wood dais next to the blue UN flag, sat three big, black leather chairs, waiting for the tribunal of judges. Facing them, rather than the prosecution team or the defense team as you would have in a North American or British courtroom, was a table for the witnesses. The prosecutors and defenders were to the sides, facing one another, though oblique to both the judges and the witness, the prosecutors to the extreme left of the judges and, like boxing the square, the defenders to the extreme right. Behind the defense sat their clients, and, back of both groups, was all the paraphernalia not so much of justice as of production. Hidden by smoked glass windows behind the prosecutors was a translation team for the converting of the proceedings into simultaneous French, English, and Kinyarwandan. Back of the defense team and behind where the defendants sat between burly guards were technicians who controlled television cameras to transmit the proceedings to monitors set in the spectator's gallery.

This gallery was a parallel room, of similar size and similar configuration, but separated from the courtroom by the wall of bulletproof glass. It was furnished with seventy-five plush theatre seats, in three rows. Fixed to each was an outlet for a headset to listen to the proceedings in the language of choice, and in clear view of each was one of the several TV monitors. I took a seat among only five visitors that morning and quickly found that I didn't need the TV monitors; it was easily possible to watch everything live. Through the glass I could plainly see the judges and, at oblique angles, both the defense and prosecution as well as the defendant between his guards. The person not so visible, however, was the witness, always with his or her back to the spectators and, if it was a sensitive witness, as a number were, they would be hidden completely behind a drawn green curtain. Then the screens as well would go blank.

It was just before nine in the morning. On the other side of the glass, things were bustling, clerks carried files, and prosecutors flapped about in their dark gowns. Across from them huddled the lawyers for the defense. It was truly an international cast. I'd learned that the prosecution team was made up of a Nigerian, a Tanzanian, and an American. The tribunal of judges, not yet present, were from Norway, Senegal, and South Africa. The defense lawyers, whom I had already met, were David Jacobs from Toronto and Ramsey Clark from New York. Through a door at the back, escorted by their guards and looking a bit confused even as they were greeted by their lawyers, entered two men I realized had to be the defendants. They were not quite what I had expected. The pastor was almost natty in a dark business suit and gold-rimmed spectacles. Gerard, the doctor, looked portly despite his five years of prison food, and wore large plastic glasses of an aviator style that had the effect of making him look bug-eyed and overly intense. They did not look like men who had come from dusty hill country villages and then spent years languishing in the clamorous boredom of a Tanzanian jail. The pastor, however, I noted on second take, did appear feeble, as he had to be helped to his seat by the guard. By this time, after all, he was seventy-eight years old. Also, the heat of the African summer notwithstanding, he was chilly—under his suit jacket he had on a wine-coloured sweater.

At nine o'clock, the clerk barked some intonation in French and everyone stood. In solemn procession, in trooped the judges. They struck a careful balance, not just in the countries they were from, but also in mix of gender (two women, Judge Navanethem Pillay from South Africa and Judge Andresia Vaz from Senegal, and a man, Eric Mose from Norway), race (one black African, Judge Vaz, one white European, Judge Mose, and one Indian, Judge Pillay), and judicial tradition (one, Judge Pillay, from a common law tradition, the other two from the civil law tradition). In their flowing black robes and brilliant red sashes, however, they resembled nothing so much as wildly exotic birds.

The trial, having started the previous autumn, was half over. The prosecution had made its case and now it was the turn of the defense. Which is what interested me. The trials going on here, like those for the Yugoslav accused, proceeding simultaneously in The Hague, were the progeny of the Nuremberg war crimes trials at the end of the Second World War. In the dock in front of us were reputedly the most awful people in the world. Which raised the question: was there any defense to be made? Back in Toronto, an educated, presumably civilized woman I had been telling about where I was going and why had made the comment: "They should just stand them up against a wall and shoot them." Which was not an uncommon view. So despicable were the crimes the defendants were accused of that otherwise reasonable people lost the perspective it had taken millennia of civilization to impart. The vengeful urge for instant punishment threatened to overwhelm the careful requirements for due process. Yet, legal principles adhered to by much of the world expected not only due process but a presumption of innocence until proven otherwise. I had to wonder, would there truly exist possibilities for those people here? How hard would it be to prevent this from becoming a kangaroo court?

Elementary justice also provided every accused with the right to a defense. Which is again what interested me. How would you organize a defense in such cases as these? How would you go about finding your witnesses? Could people, without fear, speak up with the truth, especially if it went against the perceived wisdom? Likewise, I wanted to know, if you were a defense lawyer, what would it be that motivated you? To be the prosecutor, given the world mood by this point vis-à-vis Rwanda, would be the easy option, but a lawyer on the defense side would have to be brave. So what sort of people were attracted to that: were they idealists, rebels, iconoclasts, crackpots? When people found out you had taken on the job, how did they react to you? And, beyond that, what would it be like to defend such cases? Surely the dastardliness of the deeds one's clients were accused of must weigh heavily. Therefore, not only how did you strategize in law for your defense, but how did it *feel* to defend such people?

Loaded with such questions, I searched the Web site for the court,[2] and eventually located David Jacobs. A number of lawyers, on both the prosecution and defense sides, were Canadians, possibly because of the matter of language, Rwanda's official European language being French. Jacobs was one such Canadian. I called him up and made an appointment to see him in Toronto. Forty-nine years old and a respected member of the Ontario defense bar, he had been born in Cardiff, Wales, where his father was a doctor and the family part of a tiny Jewish community. They had moved to Canada when Jacobs was sixteen. He had a leftish reputation, among other things having once been chair of the civil liberties section for the Canadian Bar Association as well as an active member of Canada's social democratic party, the NDP. His office was in a working-class and heavily ethnic section of the city; downstairs was a Portuguese restaurant. However, though he might be a lefty, he wasn't frumpy. His office was stylish, as was his dress. Hefty pieces of Inuit sculpture adorned coffee tables in the waiting area of the office, the walls of which were painted a soft, custard yellow, and he liked, I noted right away, very nice suits as well as the most up-to-date rimless eyeglasses. I learned, by the by, that we had once attended the same college, though a year apart.

Jacobs ushered me into a small corner office where both of us negotiated our way across a floor littered with briefcases, travelling bags, and stacks of transcripts and papers. He had never done any international trials before, having inherited this case when Gerard Ntakirutimana's first lawyer, a Californian, had become ill. But since then, he had thrown himself into the project, juggling his Canadian workload so much that he worried it might suffer. He was easy to talk to, had bountiful opinions and no hesitancy about taking the time to bring a visiting stranger up to speed with what was going on at the moment. He had not been involved very long but it was long enough for him to have become frustrated. Though this was our first meeting, we talked for a long time about a litany of complaints he had about everything from how the defense was viewed in the UN court system to practical problems like getting access to witnesses and getting paid. One sore point was the way defense lawyers who tapped in for their remuneration to a kind of UN legal aid system were expected to carry their own sizable expenses while waiting for the UN to process their bills. Jacobs said he'd had to mortgage his house to give him sufficient cash to keep paying for his trips back and forth to Africa to see his client and attend court.

Eventually, I looked at my notebook and spotted the question I had underlined as important to ask if only to get it out of the way. "When you are a defense attorney, two things are possible," I said, "either you've got guilty clients but you represent them because that's what our system demands. Or you believe your client is innocent. Which is it here?"

"These men," Jacobs stated flatly, "didn't do the acts they're accused of."

10

MISSIONARIES FOR JUSTICE

*I*N A LITTLE LESS THAN A YEAR, David Jacobs had travelled six times between Toronto and Arusha, Tanzania. Before the trial would end, he would make more than that number of trips again. It is an arduous journey taking about twenty hours: Toronto to Amsterdam, the inevitable wait for a connecting flight, then Amsterdam to Kilimanjaro. My own KLM flight landed at Kilimanjaro at 8:30 in the evening. Earlier in the afternoon, four hours into the final leg of the trip, I'd been able to see the Sahara through the porthole window and, before that, the coast of Libya on the Mediterranean. Then it got dark. The airport at Kilimanjaro is as tiny as you can get and still have jumbo jets. It was built to bring in tourists wanting to visit the famous mountain and then head west to the sprawling game fields of the Serengeti. Planes from Europe land, unload, and then double back to Nairobi. We exited down a stairs and had to walk fifty metres across the tarmac to a sprightly little terminal building. The night air was spectacular.

It was about forty kilometres from the Kilimanjaro airport to Arusha town. I wangled a ride in a van already almost fully loaded with French tourists, three couples eager to spend the next few days looking at elephants rather than being back home voting in the Chirac–Le Pen runoff presidential election. As we set off, they chattered merrily about what they expected to see while the two young men driving us described bird migrations—storks the previous week. The trip took forty minutes longer than I had expected, due to our having to turn down a horribly rutted road to get the French couples to their lodge. Finally, in the pitch black of 10:00 p.m., the minibus made it to my destination, a spot right in town called the Ilboro Safari Lodge. As I reached the desk, David Jacobs and an entourage of his colleagues from the defense team were just returning from supper.

The entire Ntakirutimana defense team was registered at the Ilboro. Though not by any stretch "fancy," this was indeed a pleasant place, a series of thatched huts set among flower beds and renting for about fifty dollars a night. The next morning, Sunday, I entered the dining room to find Ramsey and Georgia Clark alone at breakfast. I reintroduced myself and they shifted over so I could join them. A television perched on one of the tables was tuned to CNN and broadcasting the French elections. Ramsey Clark was seventy-four years old, four years younger than his client, the pastor. He'd had a lengthy career, starting, more than forty years earlier, as something of a wunderkind in American law and politics. His father, from Texas, had been a Supreme Court justice appointed by Truman. Then, in the 1960s, with the election of John F. Kennedy, young Ramsey got a position as assistant to the president's brother, attorney general Robert Kennedy. When Lyndon Johnson took the place of the assassinated JFK, he asked Clark himself to become attorney general, a position from which he was to guide far-reaching and even revolutionary civil rights propositions into law. During those years, the Clarks were at the epicentre of Washington action and power. Georgia Clark, who, now in her seventies and married to Ramsey for fifty-three years, still looked, with long hair falling over her shoulders, like an unreconstructed hippy, told a little anecdote as we ate our eggs about having danced with John Kenneth Galbraith. In the decades since, however, much had changed. Clark's liberalism and passion for civil liberties had carried him into worlds ever further removed from the predictable safety of the conventional. He had become associated with quixotic—some said odious—causes like the legal plight of former

Yugoslav strongman Slobodan Milosevic, Liberian dictator Charles Taylor, and Saddam Hussein, whom he had visited a number of times in Iraq in those days well before the US invasion of that country. I was naturally intrigued. When you sat down with Saddam Hussein, I asked, what did you talk about? Clark looked at me. "Saddam was very interested in Lyndon Johnson," he answered. "Though not so much his presidency as his earlier career in Texas when he had been instrumental in the whole issue of rural electrification. One of Saddam's achievements had been to deliver electric power to the back corners of Iraq and he felt that by having done so he and Johnson shared something in common." Clark's critics, of whom there was legion, finding him straying ever more outside the conventional borders (he was at that time heading up a petition to ask that George W. Bush be impeached), were having a field day in their attempts to paint him as a crackpot. "The war criminal's best friend," *Salon* magazine had sneered in 1999. Yet, in person, he was anything but wacky. To sit down with him for breakfast was like communing with Abraham Lincoln.

The Clarks had been in Arusha for three weeks. The regimen of work, now that the defense end of the trial was underway, was gruelling. On top of it—or because of it—Ramsey had developed a skin condition, a rash and itch that kept him awake nights and were reportedly driving him crazy. On afternoons after the day in court was complete, he went off with his driver, Ibrahim, to visit some doctor or another in search of a new potion that might bring relief. He'd first taken on his client, Pastor Elizaphan Ntakirutimana, back in the United States for his extradition hearing. The Ntakirutimana family, a number of whom now lived in Texas, then asked if he would continue to represent their father at his trial. The pastor was not well, Clark told me, incarceration and separation from his wife at age seventy-eight was not easy. He spent most of the time sitting in his cell, reading his bible. But Clark brightened. "He's eager to tell his story," he said, "he's been waiting a long time." He was going to put him on the stand as soon as possible, perhaps even the next day.

One by one the rest of the defense team arrived for breakfast. David Jacobs, Phil Taylor, Cynthia Hernandez, and Maurice Nsabimana. Immediately they settled into a kind of impromptu meeting. Though it was Sunday, there was a great deal of work to be done to prepare for the resumption of the trial the next morning and they had a full day planned, including a meeting with their clients, the pastor and the doctor, out at the prison on the edge of town. David Jacobs had promised me full access but it quickly became clear this did not include tagging along to the prison. The rules forbade contact with outsiders other than their lawyers. Though I would see them in court, I would never directly meet or speak to their clients. So, in due course, after everybody else had departed, I found myself alone with Maurice Nsabimana.

We carried our cups of coffee to a small table in the garden and sat facing one another. "My father," Maurice told me straight off, "was murdered." Maurice was Rwandan, but not simply Rwandan, he was a Hutu, thirty years old, pudgy with a round face and frizzy hair teased out into a modest Afro. He had big, round eyes and an intelligent, serious demeanour. He was a computer geek and Internet fanatic, and, like some member of the old beat generation or a dissident intellectual, liked to dress completely in black. This morning he wore a T-shirt (black) bearing an Internet company logo. The death of his father, eight years earlier, had been the apex of the triangle that to this point had formed his life. His father, a strict army man, was chief of military staff for the president of Rwanda, Habyirimana, and on April 6, 1994, was part of the entourage flying home from the meetings with the opposition in Tanzania when the fateful plane was shot out of the sky. Then twenty-two years old and enrolled in a college in London, Maurice had been preparing to travel to Belgium, where he anticipated a visit from his father. Instead, his mother and sisters arrived in a panic, fleeing for their lives. Up until then, the family had been living a life of privilege, part of the comfortable elite of their small country. After April 6, everything was different. In the years since, Maurice, with his mother and sisters, had remained in exile, which was fortunate for them. Their extended family who had stayed in Rwanda were wiped out of existence, completely exterminated by the Tutsi revenge.

Exile, however, though physically safe, was still a kind of house arrest, a limbo in which a young man like Maurice found it hard to be content. He was agitated, consumed with recovering something of his life and with trying to make sense of history and his family's role in it. Influenced mightily by this personal and family experience, he was in possession of two very strongly held views. One was that what had happened in Rwanda in 1994 was not a Hutu power putsch, but a Tutsi coup engineered with international support. His second firmly held position was that "if my father had lived, he would have been able to deter the slaughter in the weeks after the plane crash."

Maurice Nsabimana was not alone at the tribunal, but a kind of first among equals. Like lost and angry children, numerous Hutu Rwandans circled around the camps of the defense teams. You could see them in the halls of the court complex, disdained in no small measure by the officials busy with the prosecution of their compatriots. If they were lucky, they got short-term jobs with various defense teams that provided them some income as well as, more important to them, securing them an active role in the sorting out of history. Maurice had been named "legal assistant" to Clark, which included, among other things, making sure the interpretation coming from the translation booth during the trial was accurate. The translation, he avowed, was frequently problematic. "One witness," he told me, "had described how a defendant had 'shot at a person' but from the microphone of the translator we were told he had 'shot a person'." In the broader picture, as well, Maurice had become a confirmed skeptic. He was in thick with the gathering group of Hutu Rwandans increasingly firm in their belief that nothing could now be trusted, among which they counted the United Nations tribunal. In their view, the new regime running things in their country, the Tutsi government, was calling the shots for this court. In order to fuel and buttress their arguments, they trolled the Internet's endless stash of newspapers and magazines. Opinion and research were then starting to appear from academic circles as well as in journalism and these findings were all instantly forwarded by people like Maurice to an ever-widening circle of contacts, becoming part of the campaign to keep the debate fresh, to promote the contrarian view and battle what much of the world had accepted, the stranglehold of RPF hegemony. From his small apartment in Brussels, he had pushed forward the case and he continued to do so living out of a suitcase in Arusha. This, political and historical counterbalance, had become his mission.

The next morning in court, Phil Taylor slid into the chair beside me in the visitor gallery. The pastor himself, in what would be an all-day affair, had taken the stand—just as Ramsey Clark had promised—and Clark was taking him through the early period of his life. He'd been born in a grass hut, he testified, but had been fortunate to fall under the care of the missionaries who had made sure he got some schooling. Taylor, wiry and red-haired, had grown up in California and served in the US Marine Corps. Now he lived in Toronto and struck me right off as the kind of character you might find in some Dashiell Hammett story. While the prosecution had all the machinery of international police and justice at their finger-tips, the defense had to scramble to get their evidence and their witnesses. To assist in their investigations, or to even *have* investigations, they had to turn to freelance gumshoes like Taylor who could operate with moxie and inventiveness, not to mention on the cheap. While the judges and prosecu-tors were UN employees collecting United Nations salaries, each defense counsel was paid from an international legal aid fund that had definite limits to it, bringing to mind Kafka's observation about the defense being not so much a right as what the system tolerates. The prosecution staff had generous housing allowances and business-class airplane tickets to ferry them back and forth to Europe, but people like Taylor lived in fleabag hotel rooms out of suitcases. Or sometimes not: leaving Toronto for this trip, he had arrived at the airport too late and the agent had refused to accept his luggage. He was making do with only what he had carried on and newly purchased items like T-shirts and jeans he had managed to pick up from vendors on the streets of Arusha. Yet he appeared to thrive both in the lifestyle and on the challenges. He had worked for several of the Rwanda defense lawyers, in the process coming to know as much about central Africa as anybody. Taylor told a good story and liked books, which moved me to advise him that he himself ought to consider becoming some kind of John le Carré writer. He laughed and said he would stick with the footloose and somewhat unconventional aspect of his present employment. His main job was to line up witnesses, which involved finding them, checking their stories, and then making sure they showed up and were kept safe during their time at the trial—a task that, again, for the defense side of things came off as immeasurably more difficult than it was for the prosecution. Taylor added to the skepticism already prevalent among the defense group about the potential guilt of their clients. Like Jacobs and Clark, he had a hard time accepting the pastor as somebody possessing such deep passions that he could have perpetrated the lurid crimes of which he was accused. "He was a real church guy," he told me in a protesting voice.

The defense—at least in this case—not only believed the narrative of their clients, they did more. They bought into the Hutu version of Rwandan history. In the aftermath of the events of 1994, fed substantially by such reportage as Philip Gourevich's book, conventional wisdom about Rwanda had gelled promptly and with a uniform analysis: genocide had happened, Tutsis were victims, Hutus were evil. The power of this take overwhelmed all reporting out of Rwanda and was responsible for creating the exalted platform from which the United Nations now presumed to dispense its justice. Without denying that horrible things had happened and that hundreds of thousands lay dead, the defense and their acolytes like Maurice Nsabimana not only required but actually espoused an infinitely more nuanced version, one they seemed to believe passionately would be vindicated by history. As for myself as a writer, I knew I was caught in the middle and needed to approach these highly charged matters warily. I possess a natural skepticism for any conventional wisdom that appears too certain, yet, in wanting to keep an open mind, I also needed to be alert about who I was travelling with—lest Stockholm Syndrome set in. For the most part, I was desperately interested to find out what kind of world the accused in front of me, the people being defended in such a dedicated manner by Jacobs and Clark, were coming from. What, for example, did Taylor mean by describing the pastor as a "real church guy"?

The Seventh Day Adventist Church was founded in 1866 by a small group of zealous Christians who believed, among other things, that the Sabbath ought to be observed on Saturday. Today it boasts fifteen million members in 229 countries. Decidedly not what one might call mainstream, it is still one of the fastest growing Christian churches in the world, known for aggressive missionary work accompanied by construction of hospitals and schools in such places as Rwanda. And for people like the

Ntakirutimanas, it had provided earthly as well as spiritual salvation. Although he had been born poor, in the grass hut, the pastor had the fortune to be absorbed at an early age into the circle of this church. Eventually, he became one of the first generation of black Africans to take charge of its local leadership. As he recounted his story on the stand in the courtroom, all the old mission terminology was present in his language: "secretary, field office, division, conference." Through his long life, it seemed, he had applied himself to his job, kept his nose clean, and, by the time he was sixty, had become a supervising official, a position of considerable local status, and three of his own children were trained as doctors. Yet that life, by all accounts, was far from grand. The Adventists are conservative, modest, and pious. In no country, including Rwanda, is it axiomatic that they are part of the power structure in the ways Catholic or Anglican churches and officials might be. They reputedly disdain politics. The pastor, whether you went by the accounts of others or simply observed him in court, was a stern, uninteresting man, not so much a church leader in the charismatic or political sense—as the prosecution had spent its weeks trying to establish—as in the accounting sense. The pastor, as Taylor had gone on to explain, was a fastidious bean counter. "When he was put in charge of thirty-four churches, a hospital, and a couple of schools, his main task was to keep the books."

As Clark took him through the events of his life, he explained how the church consumed his life: each morning he travelled to his simple office, got on his knees for a lengthy period of prayer, then spent the rest of the long day making sure the church's machinery was efficiently and honestly run. Which raised for me the same skepticism it had for Jacobs, Clark, and Phil Taylor; where, one had to wonder, was there room or time or inclination for the almost unthinkable deeds of which he was accused? Maurice had brought me a copy of the indictment and I read over the list of accusations. Did he and his son really do these things? And then, if they had done even some of them, what was there? Evil? Cowardice? I found it perplexing. I felt the same way about Maurice and the story he'd related about his father and his family; was that the whole truth? Where was truth? Who had actually done what, or mandated what? With Rwanda, it seemed perfectly possible to believe either or both sides. With all the dead bodies square in the middle.

Ramsey Clark, looking a bit like the TV lawyer, Matlock, continued to lead the pastor through the story of his life. In a courtroom that was over-whelmingly European and educated-class African, Clark, with his Texas drawl, introduced a kind of folksiness. The head of the prosecution team, Charles Adeogun-Phillips, was a Nigerian educated in the UK and came across as accordingly imperious; the presiding judge, Eric Mose, a slim, helpful-looking man with sandy hair and glasses who did all the talking for the bench, at least during that stage of witness examination, was Norwe-gian, an urbane Scandinavian. Though Clark had spent his adult life in Washington and New York, he seemed to eschew the worldliness on which all those others bustling about in the court looked to thrive. His aspect of the story was intriguing: the former attorney general of the United States at age seventy-four had come all this way to defend a man, seventy-eight, of his own generation but with a completely opposite life.

At noon, the court broke for lunch and the lawyers headed downstairs to the cubbyhole offices they had been given one floor below. There was work for them to do, phone calls and faxes to deal with, provided the outgoing lines were working. Cynthia Hernandez had spent the morning trying to get hold of a witness, a Seventh Day Adventist Church official from California, who, Clark hoped, might say a few good things about the pastor. After the events of 1994, the church had carried out its own inves-tigation and declared that nobody in its employ had done anything wrong. But Cynthia had to announce they were not going to be able to get a visa for him in time to be of any use. She had also laid out lunch—samosas, bread, and cheese. "The beef ones," said Clark, "are the best." I noticed on his desk a well-thumbed copy of the Gourevitch book, *We Regret to Inform You That Tomorrow We Will Be Killed with Our Families.* "Indictment by book," he muttered.

I decided to take the lunch break as an opportunity to explore and see if I could get around the building without becoming lost, though two days in, I was starting to acquire some sense of direction. The first thing I found was a washroom where, by the sink, was hung a big wire basket filled with foil-wrapped condoms. Back out in the hall, I regrettably did find myself promptly lost and had to have a guard turn me around and point me in the right direction. I thought I would seek out the United Nations' public relations office and pick up some material about the court. I didn't have to go that far. Mounting a walkway, I passed a wall loaded with United Nations promotional material. On large posters were explanations, in English and French, of what lay behind the tribunal: the mandate—Resolution 955 of the Security Council. A definition of genocide. An explication of the trial chambers and the appeals court; how judges, who could apply from any member state, were elected to four-year terms; how the prosecutor, at the time Carla del Ponte, an Italian, worked out of offices in Arusha and Kigali, the Rwandan capital. There was a prominently displayed message from the registrar, since January 2001, Adama Dieng of Senegal: "Justice is no longer local, it is going global." Then a final poster citing the "Achievements of the ICTR," itemizing how it had arrested more than seventy individuals and convicted Prime Minister Jean Kambanda (the first time for a head of government). It all added up to one overwhelming message: this was not a court like any other. What other court in the world, I thought, would dare mount a public relations campaign that boasted of its overwhelming conviction rate? Like the extension of some police department, the tribunal gave off an irrefutable sense of its own certainty, it had the bad guys and needed only to go through the motions.

Back upstairs in the spectator's gallery, I settled in for the afternoon and commenced chatting with the person occupying the next chair, an Irish woman with a great pad of paper on her knee, Rosemary Byrne. Byrne told me she was a law professor who directed something called the International Process and Justice Project at Trinity College, Dublin, and had been coming to the trial every day. Both as an academic and a jurist, she had an abundance of interest in how this court was working. In the Hague, the UN was moving at that very moment to set up an international criminal court that would be permanent. But there were a multitude of questions about how it would work. Even basic questions had not yet been settled, such as which legal traditions it might work from, a court, after all, being nothing if not the embodiment of the mores and traditions of the community over which it presides. In a sense this tribunal appeared to be serving as a kind of dry run for the oncoming permanent court. Its strengths would be noted but so would its mistakes, not, it was hoped, to be repeated. Other important things for a court are consistency and predictability, and to this end Rosemary Byrne was watching the interactions between the counsel and the judges. I could see her pen scribble whenever one happened; she recorded objections, interruptions, motions. Most interjections originated from the Norwegian Judge Mose.

So far, Judge Mose's colleagues—the two women, Judge Navanethem Pillay from South Africa and Andresia Vaz from Senegal—had not uttered a word. There were three tribunals operating simultaneously and, according to Byrne, their flavour and effectiveness depended entirely on the personnel selected to staff them. There was "a vast difference one to the next largely dependent on the nationality and judicial traditions of those participating." If a court wasn't run with a firm and fair hand, all kinds of chaos could erupt and carry things either into farce or danger. There had been an example of this a few days earlier in this very courtroom, a skirmish after which the defense had filed a motion alleging "prosecutorial misconduct." For the incident in question, the witness had been a young Adventist preacher, the star, Phil Taylor told me, of their church. The problem came when the Nigerian prosecutor, Charles Adeogun-Phillips, rose to cross-examine. Within minutes he was accusing the witness of lying about his identity and then of being wanted for raping three women. Objections flew fast and furious. No corroborating evidence was offered and the judges intervened to ask what kind of "fishing expedition" the prosecutor might be on. Ramsey Clark was near apoplectic: "Your Honour, this is the most unprofessional cross-examination I have ever heard," he had fumed.

The problem, however, quickly became even more complicated. In the gallery that afternoon was a reporter from Inter-news AllAfrica.com, and by suppertime the story had flashed back to Rwanda and the rest of Africa: "Defense Witness Wanted in Kigali for Genocide, Prosecutor Alleges." This sent the defense into paroxysms, not just about the surprise and what they believed were absurd allegations, but about what the broadcast would mean for the safety of their witness and his family, hidden away in an Arusha safe house. Despite the fact that witness identities were kept carefully secret, back in their place of exile (and back in Rwanda), people would put two and two together and know immediately who they were. When they contacted people to be witnesses, Phil Taylor told me, "the first thing they ask is for confirmation they will be safe."

A few days later, a second issue highlighting the clash of traditions came up. Prosecutor Phillips produced a statement allegedly from an eighty-three-year-old woman who had travelled with the Ntakirutimanas during their flight from Rwanda. She was a witness neither for the prosecution, who argued she was too old and too ill, nor for the defense, who, as Taylor explained, couldn't expose her to the risk of calling her out of Kigali, where she now lived. But in 1995, investigators had questioned her and produced notes, which the prosecutor now introduced. A brouhaha erupted with Jacobs jumping up to object to the statement being submitted "as if testimony." "It's just a bunch of words on a piece of paper," Ramsey Clark protested.

After a hasty conference, the judges ruled to allow the statement. I looked over at Rosemary Byrne, who was scribbling furiously. "If this were a jury trial," she said at the break, "this would be very prejudicial." Here, though, it seemed to be a pattern for "judges to allow pretty much everything because they'll be the ones making the ultimate judgment."

Also in the spectator's gallery that afternoon was a plump, friendly-looking blonde woman, who took the seat on the other side of me. Eventually she introduced herself: Mrs Mose, wife of the judge. She too was a lawyer, with a practice back in Norway, which she had given up to be here in Africa with her husband and to supervise their adolescent children. They'd been living in Arusha, part of the United Nations community, for a couple of years. How did she like it? "Life here can be a bit boring," she averred. For their children, who went to an international school, it was an interesting, once-in-a-lifetime experience, but for her, time hung heavy, a highlight being the opportunity to play bridge in a club that had roots going all the way back to colonial days. What she really liked was the opportunity to sit in on the trials and watch her husband at work. This particular trial, she said, she found very interesting. She had been reading, she told me, the Gourevitch book. She thought it very powerful. "I hope you won't write anything critical," she mused, upon learning that I too was a writer. "They get so much criticism. And my husband works so hard."

11

THE GENEVA OF AFRICA

*I*N 2000, DURING THE LAST SUMMER of his presidency, Bill Clinton travelled to Africa. It was, in many respects, a journey of contrition as well as, arguably, the beginning of what turned into a new round of big power G8 concern about 'whither Africa'. Wanting to try to get things started with a clean slate, Clinton expressed careful regrets about the slavery that had taken so many Africans forcefully to the Americas and, as well, stated his regrets about Rwanda. Then he visited Arusha. Given a tour of the ICTR and duly impressed with this symbol of international judicial effort, the US president correspondingly pronounced Arusha "the Geneva of Africa."

Though local officials wasted no time getting the presidential phrase printed as a slogan on the outside wall of the International Conference Center, Tanzanians in general might have been less certain they wanted to be so compared. One wag mused as to whether the inverse could ever happen: a sign in Geneva calling it "the Arusha of Europe." But the significant thing is that whenever something so substantial comes to, or is imposed on, a community, a number of questions naturally open up, and Arusha was no exception. Every day in Ibrahim's white Chevrolet, which he kept immaculately clean and maintained, we would bump down the road from our hotel. First we would pass through our immediate neighbourhood, people and goats and huts and shops all impinging on the broken-up and potholed road, then turn on the main thoroughfare and head into town for a session of the court. If it were in America or Britain, Arusha would be called a "farming town." It had long been a market centre for a region where crops of coffee, maize, and wheat were grown on the sunny plain shaded by the towering Mount Meru and just beyond the shadow of Kilimanjaro. The sprawling game grounds of the Serengeti and Ngorongoro Crater stretched to the west, attracting their throngs of tourists. The local people, however, were not great fans of the game animals, which threatened to either trample their crops or eat them. Rather than the tourist hotels, what they prized was their local economy and its symbol in their community, the International Conference Center donated to Tanzania and Arusha by the friendly government of China. Yet it was this that they had now lost, it having been transformed, with the dispatch that global will and committed money can achieve, from a centre representative of local or national trade into a gigantic judicial complex for the rest of the world.

When the UN blew into town, some locals, like Ibrahim, had benefited at least economically. By opting to go into business hiring out himself and his car, he and his wife had prospered. Ibrahim was a devout Christian (despite his name, he was not Muslim, though there were Muslims in Arusha and every morning I would be wakened at 5:00 a.m. by a muezzin loudspeaker calling the faithful to prayer). Yet, so industrious and conscientious was he that even on a Sunday morning on his way to church, he would call by to deliver any of his clients who needed a lift. But though he personally had benefited from the influx of the outsiders, as he had watched the town change he remained far from certain it was all for the general good. "With the UN coming," he said, "prices for everything immediately shot skyward, housing costs going up by as much as 500%." As Arusha became the Geneva of Africa, it had turned, for many of its own citizens, into an alien, more expensive place.

The changes wrought by the arrival of the ICTR were both social and economic. By importing a large staff, the project had increased the local population. It had funnelled money into the community. The United Nations was spending almost $100 million a year on the tribunal, and though not all this cash remained in Arusha by any means—even the salaries of most of the people based there were probably banked back in their home countries—enough stuck to make an impact. The predominant theory about economic benefit in such cases is the "trickle-down" theory: the people bringing in money spend it, those receiving it in the first round from them then spend it yet again. In a cycle of diminishing, though ever more widely spread, increments, the money makes its way through the economy, its impact being felt several times over. Ibrahim and the hotel staff at the Ilboro benefited, without question. The dozens of locals who had been hired as guards and secretaries and groundskeepers and drivers and cleaners at the court complex likewise benefited. Some did substantially well: there were Tanzanian lawyers on the prosecutorial staff, for example, pulling world-level salaries. All the places these people went to do their shopping benefited. However, the inflationary theory accompanies the trickle-down theory, and here, for the community at large, as Ibrahim had pointed out, the economic effect was arguably as disruptive as it was beneficial. What did it mean if you managed to get some kind of job but everything you were accustomed to purchasing now cost five times what it had previously? What did it mean if you had to pay these prices *without* benefiting from having received a job?

Similarly, the social effects had the potential to be disruptive. The ICTR had several hundred employees, some of them local but a good many imported either on a long-term basis, like the sitting judges and their families, or on a rotating, transient basis like the defense lawyers. Both these groups created disruption in the existing social structure. Arusha already had a black Tanzanian and an Asian or east Indian elite in its local political and business structure. But, like the arrival in the past of colonial governors and their hangers-on, the UN lathered on a new or additional elite. The judges, prosecutors, and upper-level UN officials possessed both high incomes and high status. They would either infiltrate the existing elite and possibly, with their numbers, overwhelm it, or more likely and failing that, they would become a parallel, competing elite.

The foreign employees, especially at the top levels of judges and prosecutors with high salaries and generous expense allowances, hived themselves off into the kinds of expatriate suburban enclaves every African city has in one form or another, rented villas with walls and security gates, limitless domestic staffs of cooks and gardeners and night guards. They and their families could be seen booting around town, chauffeured by their hired drivers. In short order a chasm between them and all but the thinnest upper crust of local society followed as they demanded and were provided with their own schools for their foreign children, their own clubs and restaurants catering to the kind of money they had to spend, their own life. Many African cities have such enclaves of foreigners, but so many high-level UN people had all arrived so abruptly in Arusha, they had caused a substantial impact.

The stratification worked not only at the elite levels, but then all the way down the social ladder in sequence of the positions: judges and prosecutors at the top, then high-level UN functionaries like the director of public relations and the officials in the office of the registrar, then on down through stenographers and translators, security guards and cleaners. This was the rigid hierarchy inside the court complex when everybody was at work, and would be so after-hours out in the community as well.

The chasms could be seen everywhere, even within what one might have thought were tightly knit communities. The lawyers, for example, inhabited a universe that was proscribed and contained inside the structure of the task they had to accomplish—the cases and the trials. But it was not the same world for the defense lawyers as it was for the colleagues they faced every day, those who worked for the UN. The defense were transient freelancers who lived out of suitcases and worked out of their briefcases. The prosecutors, by contrast, had their offices and permanent staff inside the court complex and their proper homes in the enclave of expatriate families with colonial-style amenities. I observed the gulf this created at the same time as I watched the longing, particularly on the part of someone like David Jacobs, to bridge it. Yet it would never be possible. Phil Taylor, who tended to see the other side as the enemy, was not bothered in the least by having nothing to do with the UN people. If we were eating lunch and a prosecutorial staff person were at the next table, Phil would shift his chair ever so slightly in order to show his back. But Jacobs came from a world where at the end of the day a lawyer was a lawyer, class and professional collegiality overcoming the adversarial moments of the courthouse and the workday. He did not like the distance that had been created here; in fact, he chafed at it. One night the wall briefly came down. At a restaurant in the middle of town, run by an expatriate Australian, the steaks were perfectly done, the imported wine flowed freely. In the corner was a piano where, after two drinks, David perched himself and commenced running jazzy excursions up and down the keyboard. Sitting at the bar as well that evening were a couple of lawyers I knew to be from the prosecution, a tall American and a German woman. Within minutes they slid off their bar stools and gravitated to the piano to join David. He looked up and across his face I could see splayed a broad smile of happiness. But half an hour later, everyone had to depart. We, back to the Ilboro, the prosecution lawyers to the expatriate compound. Our separate worlds.

But all outsiders, ultimately, were transient. I, as a short-term visitor, inhabited a precise and precious world, pretty much limited to the hotel, my little cottage with the mosquito netting over the bed, the dining room for breakfast, the gardens overwhelmed with their riot of flowers and exotic plants. Inside that world the nightly irritation of the barking neighbourhood dogs was offset by the unremitting cheerfulness of Flora and Agnes, the women who managed the front desk. My life was circumscribed, my material possessions limited by the space I had in my luggage and the things I had chosen to bring with me, my schedule confined by the date and time written on my return air ticket. All outsiders, even the judges for the tribunal, though their stay was longer and they inhabited fancy houses instead of a hotel room and had a bigger luggage, lived some version of this. They too knew they would some day have to leave. And what would be left then would be the Arusha for whom the court and the international attention and all the high-flying, passing-through celebrities were more of an irritant than a necessity. The other Arusha.

Desiring to get some sense of this other Arusha, I set off one morning on foot through the gates of the Ilboro and turned toward town. Africans will call a place a town even though it might be in fact a small city. Arusha, at that point, had about 270,000 people, but was still called "a town" by every local voice. The thing is that in Africa, urban centres, even when they are huge cities like Dar Es Salaam or Nairobi or Kampala, retain many aspects of country. So to designate something a town, that intermediate stage between country and city, can be appropriate. Sociologists and political scientists who are beginning to study the urbanization of Africa have recognized this, and have taken to using another term to describe a substantial aspect of the rapidly growing urban centres: "informal." This, though a broad term, has proven an accurate and useful choice of language. The organization of urban entities, as I had noted in the shantytowns in Nairobi, is not strict, either in law or in the elements of planning, and into the vacuum so created creeps 'informal'. At its worst, it means utterly devoid of either control or planning, entities like the squatter shantytowns, entire suburbs that have come together in many cities with no services, no sanitation, no utilities, no security. But even at its less extreme, what urban sociologists notice is that the grasp and control of authorities fail to encompass, in any complete way, large parts of the economy, housing, services, or land-use planning in extensive sections of African cities. The informal world that results is haphazard, spontaneous, and, of course, insecure. It is a world, according to observers like Professor Winnie Mitullah of the University of Nairobi, that operates outside of, if not directly counter to, planning controls and central management.[1] There was an "official" Arusha, a city centre of boulevards with shops and hotels and government buildings—and a charming clock tower situated on the exact halfway point between Cairo and Cape Town. It included the United Nations court complex and the suburban compounds where the international cadre lived and shopped and went to school. But for many, many black Tanzanian citizens, this world was out of reach, either as some place they might live or even as some place they might find work. To balance it—and to survive—the ordinary Tanzanian Arushans had created their parallel, unofficial, informal world.

For a couple of kilometres, I marched down a hill with a pronounced slope. The road had once been paved, but was badly maintained, deeply potholed, and, in places where the pavement had long disappeared, reclaimed completely by dirt. Should a heavy rain come, there would be close to a virtual washout. Human habitation all along the way was dense and, certainly by my North American standards, unorganized. Houses ranged in their variety from solid well-constructed dwellings with small yards to humble lean-tos stuck together in a haphazard manner, using whatever cast-off materials were available. None of them was in any way on a proper lot but what was uniform was that each had a scorch of earth and a cooking pot in front. Everything was pushed forward, toward the road, by an avalanche of vegetation, trees and plants and vines and gardens. This variety in itself made things feel like the city and the country both at the same time. Bits of farming went on wherever people felt like doing so or could manage a clear plot of ground; patches of maize, beans, coffee, tomatoes flourished behind people's houses. It appeared that almost every family was supplying its own produce needs, as well, perhaps, as some extra to sell. Rickety stands staffed by women or children lined whole stretches of the roadside. Many of the houses, by the same token, served as more than just residences. In a front room or on a front stoop would be set up some kind of shop: shoe repair, sewing, selling of vegetables or soft drinks, butcheries, and, as I got down toward the bottom and closer to the main highway, hair shops. These offered both simple barbering as well as more elaborate women's beauty services like hair extensions and the intricate cornrow braiding that was popular throughout Arusha. As I approached the highway, these increased in number so that eventually there were so many of them they stood chockablock, making me wonder how there could be enough business to sustain so many of the same kind of shop. There had been a great scramble to find distinctive names: muscular monikers like Mama Defender Hair Salon stood next door to unconscious semi-bloopers like Public Hair Salon.

Branching off from this essentially main artery was a network of more simple trails. Immediately I was in territory that was much quieter, less commercial, more pastoral and agricultural. A few cows and chickens and no vehicular traffic whatsoever, only people on bicycles or ambling on foot. It was night and day in contrast to the other road; the noise decibel level dropped by 70%. A placid young girl of about twelve came toward me with a huge bunch of green bananas balanced on her head. I encountered more people, all of them exceedingly friendly and courteous to this obviously strange visitor, pausing to nod and greet me: *"Jambo,"* the casual Swahili greeting, or *"Habari, muzuri,"* the more formal one.

The word that popped into my head to describe it all was "picturesque," which instantly made me realize how frozen I was into being a visiting North American who could never escape the role of tourist. As if to challenge the issue even further, from behind a bunch of trees around a bend in the trail came three young Masai men. Of indeterminate age, wrapped in red blankets, wide feet in sandals, loopy earlobes, they marched toward me, picking their teeth with long sticks. All were laughing at something, which I hoped was not me but perhaps rather some private joke. Yet, I was again overcome by an automatic response I was powerless to avoid. In my mind's eye I had already framed them, these three marching toward me with the lush greenery behind them and the cars whizzing by on the highway below. What a great picture! The urge to photograph was like a caffeine hit, so strong it made me jumpy. My mind raced over the things I would have to do: I would have to negotiate, after stopping them and through jabbering and hand signals explaining my intention, I'd have to make some bargain. Only then could I get them to pose and snap the picture. Having such thoughts depressed me. What a menace the white man like me can be, I thought, what a pest. How unable to simply take the beauty of a moment for what it was. The Masai men and I met and passed. *"Jambo,"* I said. They said something in Masai, and then I could hear them break into giggles and some kind of spitting noises. I kept walking, not daring to turn and look back.

I could not have taken a photo of the Masai men, anyway, I was not carrying my camera. By this time I had learned a harsh lesson and that was to leave that piece of what, in much of my life, was essential equipment back in my room. African people, I'd discovered through a series of uncomfortable encounters, did not like to have their pictures taken. At least, not out on the road or in the street. If they knew you, of course, it would be another matter. Flora and Agnes and the other clerks at the hotel begged to have their photos taken and would position themselves either professionally behind the reception desk or posing coquettishly by the flower beds. But there was a reciprocity, the understanding being that I would mail them the prints. Out on the road, the reactions were invariably negative, sometimes hostile; if people didn't yell at you or throw things, they would demand money. Even children did so with a kind of snide brashness. They knew no fair exchange was about to happen; all a local would see was another *muzungu* stealing an image. Tourist photography was just one example of outsider invasion. The relationship created by the visiting tourist from behind his camera or—even worse—his video recorder, could easily be construed as larcenous and exploitative, turning grinding daily life into something quaint to take back home and show his friends while giving nothing in return. You couldn't blame the locals for becoming irritated; go take a picture of the animals in the game park, they might rightfully tell you, the woman weeding her tomato patch did not wish to become a souvenir.

There was one photograph, though, that I really did want to have and I began to scheme how to get it. I wanted a picture of the jail where the prisoners from Rwanda were being detained. I thought it would be an important supplement to the article I was intending to write about the trial as well as a significant document in the record of the UN project in Arusha. The lawyers, who had visited frequently, described the jail as not a dungeon by any means but a fairly comfortable place. The UN wing had been recently constructed, the cells were clean, the detainees were allowed to wear their own clothes—suits and ties for some of them, David had told me—they had access to books, television, and even Internet, and there was an exercise yard. But the prison could not be photographed. Under the catch-all rubric of "security considerations," this was a sort of general rule in a number of countries. If you were caught trying to photograph a jail, the punishment could be severe. Which made the challenge seem even greater.

I developed a plan. The prison where the Rwanda detainees were held was along the highway heading out of the west side of town, past a stretch of hotels and restaurants and outdoor markets and just at the beginning of fields of maize and pastureland. Across the road was the local airport. This was not the international airport where my flight had come from Amsterdam, but one for local and charter flights, small planes. This airport, however, as all airports, had a control tower and a roof accessible by a set of outside stairs. This roof was the kind of place where people who had nothing better to do might go just to watch the planes take off and land. Up there, I thought, might I not get a surreptitious snap?

Left in the restaurant after lunch when the lawyers had gone off to court, I proposed my plan to Georgia and Ibrahim. Georgia thought it would be an adventure and begged to come along. Ibrahim looked worried, though he eventually shrugged and agreed to drive us. We climbed into his car and sailed down the road I'd walked not so long before. It was bumpy and Ibrahim had to skirt the potholes, the pedestrians, the goats and dogs and cows. At the main road we turned right and sped toward the edge of town. Before long, we reached the airport, spoke to the manager, and were up on the roof. We seemed harmless enough, a couple of goofy foreign tourists, an elderly woman and a middle-aged man with our local driver, who could only shrug helplessly at the manager in a 'what can you do with these *muzungus*' kind of manner. Out on the runways there was a dribble of activity; a couple of planes took off and one landed. I pulled my camera from my bag like a good tourist and looked around. I made a big show of getting Georgia and Ibrahim to pose with a few parked Cessnas and Mount Meru in the background. Georgia was enjoying the game and began to ham it up, contorting herself into a variety of poses. Ibrahim continued to look uncomfortable but indulgent. I pressed the shutter. Out of the corner of my eye, all the time, I kept the scene across the road, a high fence of both barbed and electrified wire, a couple of watch towers, and a collection of two-storey brick buildings. It was some distance away, boxed between a field of maize and a banana plantation. But it was there. What, I thought, adjusting my lens to full zoom, was to prevent a half turn and a casual depression of the shutter while I looked like all I was doing was checking my exposure meter?

At mid-afternoon, Georgia and I arrived back at court. We were cleared through security and made our way up to the spectator's gallery of Chamber Three. When we got to our seats, the pastor was on the stand with Ramsey leading the questions. They were moving close, in the chronological sequence of things, to April 16, the fateful day laid out in the charges filed against the Ntakirutimanas and the fateful day in the pastor's entire life. It was slated to be a traumatic episode of testimony, but just before they could get into it, the pastor waved his hand and was taken to the toilet.

When he returned, Clark introduced the morning of April 16 and asked him to recall what happened. "It was 5:30, not yet dawn," the pastor testified, "I was still in bed. Gendarmes rang the bell at my gate." The national police, four of whom had been at the mission compound for several days, brought two letters—one for him personally, and one for him to take to the *bourgmestre*, or local mayor. Clark asked him to read his letter. Taking a minute, he unfolded a piece of paper and began to read in Kinyrwandan. Into my headset came the English translation. "Our dear leader, Pastor Elizaphan Ntakirutimana, how are you?" From then on, not quite the exact words of Gourevitch's title, but close. "With our children" replaced "with our families." And instead of "help," the word "compassion" was what God, in their words, had bestowed upon the pastor. Asking for his intervention to save their lives, they thanked him in advance. But the great difference between what we heard in court and the story in the book was the pastor's reply. After a futile trip to the *bourgmestre,* Ntakirutimana penned a reply to his doomed brethren, which, in his testimony, was worded, "in conclusion, you are in God's hands." Which was different, it occurred to me, from the response gathered from hearsay accounts in Philip Gourevitch's travels through Rwanda: "God no longer wants you."

There was a moment of silence in the room, on both sides of the bullet-proof glass. The pastor was then asked to go through the seven signatories to the letter, recounting his relationship with each. Every eye in the courtroom and spectator's gallery was on him. He began in a faltering voice. "This one taught me … this one was under my authority … I taught him … this one had a sickly wife and I took him to work." He removed his glasses and brought a handkerchief to dab his eyes. It was a difficult moment, an elderly man naked with his memories. Either the man before us, I thought, is the most shameless and accomplished of actors, or his story is to be believed. Once the pastor had composed himself, Clark asked him how he felt when he read the letter the first time, on the morning eight years earlier. "That letter shattered me," he testified, "I didn't know how to conduct myself. I started trembling."

That evening, there was chaos for the defense team. Their witness, who had been accused two days earlier by the prosecutor of having killed people, was in a major spot. His testimony done, he was going to have to leave Arusha and, because of the radio broadcast, had reason to fear for the safety of himself, his wife, and small son, who had accompanied him to Arusha. Jacobs and Clark submitted a stern motion strongly criticizing the prosecutors for the carelessness of the accusations they had made. But now the matter was not just in the abstract of motions and counter-motions; the family, they believed, could truly be at risk. After court, Ramsey, David, Phil, the whole staff scrambled in a triangle that took them from the safe house where the witness family was staying to the witness protection and security office to the judge's chambers, at every stop seeking answers and reassurance. One thing their motion had asked was that the little family be put into the equivalent of a US witness protection program, sent not back to whatever African country they'd been in (probably Congo) but somewhere safe, like Europe. So incensed was Clark about the prosecutor's allegations he couldn't stand still. By 6:00 p.m., however, the judges had decided against their requests: the witnesses would not be protected longer, they could be returned to wherever they'd come from and nothing more could be done.

The next morning, when he opened his cross-examination, Charles Adeogun-Phillips told the court that he had been trying to obtain an affidavit from Philip Gourevitch and wondered if he might submit the exchange of e-mails to show his thus far unsuccessful attempts. Everybody looked at one another, puzzled. It was unclear what this was about. The author did not appear as a prosecution witness though his name was on a list. Now it seemed the prosecution wanted to vindicate a Web article in which was described the interview with the pastor in Texas. What emerged through the confusion, however, was a reminder of how much this, of all the Rwanda trials, had to do with a book. To be fair, the indictments were sworn before Gourevitch sought out and interviewed the pastor in 1996. But the book, perhaps more than anything else, had galvanized the issue—and put human dimensions to it for the public, both in America and throughout the wider world (even to Judge Mose's wife). Because everything hinged on allegation and documentation, the book and its power formed, arguably, a central part of the narrative of this trial. Yet, though that may be so, the prosecutor's attempt fizzled. The author would not be a witness either in person or through affidavit. Under cross-examination, the pastor testified he didn't know Gourevitch was a journalist. "He did not write what I told him, he wrote what he wanted," he said.

The cross-examination of Gerard turned into a bit of a free-for-all. If the doctor and his father were to be convicted, I surmised, their version of events as it had been laid out through the previous four days of testimony would have to be shown to be lies, both by the strength of the testimony of the prosecution witnesses, which had preceded them, and now by nailing them themselves in cross-examination. When Gerard told the court he spent the days after the massacre rescuing children from beside the bodies of their dead mothers and setting up an examination table in a crowded hall in order to treat an elderly man's rectal prolapse, we'd have to be persuaded beyond the shadow of a doubt he was in fact doing other, far more nasty, things. As was the pastor when he claimed to be fleeing, looking after elderly women, and praying. The prosecutors rose behind their bench, Charles Adeogun-Phillips pulling himself up to his full 6'2" and looking stern and aggrieved. "Can you help me with this?" he asked. He suggested that by fleeing as he did on the 16th of April, Gerard was abandoning his patients. David Jacobs jumped up to object to the question. The judge said, "Mr. Jacobs is right. You must reformulate." When the prosecutor made a sarcastic remark about the doctor's intelligence, Jacobs objected again. Now Judge Mose commenced to intervene more frequently. "We don't need these kinds of questions," he admonished, "we have assessed Dr Ntakirutimana and we don't need these questions about intelligence."

Then, turning to the doctor: "What is the answer to this question put a bit sharply to you, Doctor Gerard?"

What appeared to be happening was that through a combination of the aggressiveness of his questioning and the resulting objections from David Jacobs and admonishments from the bench, prosecutor Phillips failed to mount a consistent line of attack. Everything he tried got distracted and diverted. By ten o'clock, it was apparent he was getting nowhere. The doctor was answering confidently and whenever things got too pushy, Jacobs would interrupt. Judge Mose seemed to take the side of the witness and the defense, pushing Phillips to cut short whole lines of questioning and rebuking him when he was argumentative. Finally, Adeogun-Phillips gave up. He sat down, deflated. He had lost his moment, I thought.

Which brought the judges into the equation. For the next hour, the three of them took over. At some point in the middle of 2001, when they'd lost their first (and only) case, chief prosecutor Carla del Ponte complained about her staff, saying they won cases because of the judges, not the competence of the prosecutors. I thought about this, especially when Judge Pillay, the incisive South African former defense lawyer, turned on her microphone. Patiently and rigorously, she zeroed in on every statement's potential inconsistency, every hour not fully accounted for. Looking for holes.

And there it ended. The defense team gathered back in Ramsey Clark's cramped office on the second floor to commence a reassessment, the extra people spilling out into the hall. On the whole, it was agreed, they should not feel too bad. Damage assessment was done. Gerard, they agreed, had held up pretty well. At the very worst, somebody said, he could be accused of leaving his post and his patients, though he did so eight days after the foreign doctors bailed out of Mugonero. The judge asked him why he hadn't gone back (after July when he'd left for Zaire), and Phil Taylor said, "He should have said 'because I'd have been killed'." Still remaining were closing arguments, scheduled for some three months later, in August, with a verdict coming possibly in November. They had to consider a meeting to discuss these. A few of the staff wanted to hold it right away, on that very afternoon, but Clark had finally made an appointment with a Tanzanian doctor about an hour's drive away to have a look at his skin rash. David

Jacobs, after five weeks, was keen to get back to Toronto and hoped to leave that night. Perhaps, he suggested, they could schedule their meeting in Toronto or New York some time in June. That seemed to sound okay, so there, for the defense staff, the matter rested. They would all prepare to disperse. And for the doctor and the pastor, as at the end of every day in court, they were put back into shackles and handcuffs to be taken to the Tanzanian jail. Behind the maize and banana plantations. Across the road from the airport.

12

VERDICTS ON RWANDA

*I*N FEBRUARY 2003, THE NTAKIRUTIMANA JUDGMENTS came down. Guilty as charged. The doctor was convicted of genocide and crimes against humanity; the pastor of aiding and abetting genocide. Gerard was sentenced to twenty-five years in prison; the pastor, by this time seventy-eight years old, to ten years.

In Texas the Ntakirutimana family, including the pastor's wife, was distraught. By telephone I spoke to his daughter, Gloria, now working as a nurse in Laredo. "My brother and father shouldn't be where they are," she stated in a thin voice, sounding wrung out and helpless. Clark and Jacobs immediately launched an appeal.

On one level the verdicts, if correct and proper, ought to have settled things. They should have shown just punishment at long last meted out. They should have shown to victims and the vulnerable that there was indeed protection for them. They should have shown that at the end of awful happenings, impartial justice, tough but fair, can step in and make things right. The overview provided by objective evidence should have trumped narrow subjective opinion, persuading even the lawyers that the belief they held in the innocence of their clients was, in fact, misplaced and wrong. The verdicts should have been a major step in the process of the world community redeeming itself for its hideous lack of action at the moment the crisis was happening. But whether they did any of these things remained murky. Were these just punishments? Was the system truly working? Had they got the right people for the right reasons?

The tenth anniversary of the 1994 horrors came and went. Books were published. Some, like that of General Dallaire, were non-fiction memoirs; others were novels. Movies came out. Three movies, in fact, were launched as a fourth went into production. The country hardly anybody had heard of a decade earlier became seared forever on the world's consciousness. But the myth-making machinery had taken over and Rwanda became, as somebody put it, "Hollywood-ized." For so long nobody's orphan, it now was adopted by Los Angeles film producers and New York, Paris, London, and Toronto book publishers.

The UN court in Arusha, the International Criminal Tribunal for Rwanda, ploughed on ahead. The mandated end time, set for it when the first accused were brought to the Tanzanian town in late 1996, came and went. Security Council resolutions 1503 (in 2003) and 1534 (in 2004) extended the court into what was called its Third Mandate. Its budget had ballooned into the stratosphere, but still was supplied—and spent. In its report to United Nations headquarters in 2004, the ICTR reported that twenty-three trials had been completed; twenty-five more were in process; and eighteen accused still awaited trial. Fourteen persons indicted by the ICTR prosecutor were still at large, and fifteen investigations were ongoing, providing the potential for more indictments. "On the basis of the information presently available," the report stated, "it is estimated that by 2008, the Tribunal may have completed trials involving between 65 and 70 persons." Just to leave room for error, security council resolution 1503 had provided for a 2010 completion. Fourteen years after the ICTR commenced business; sixteen years after the Rwanda 'genocide'. By the way, of the twenty-three trials completed, twenty had resulted in guilty verdicts, only three in acquittals.

The real question about the International Criminal Tribunal, though, remained to be asked, and it seemed it might have to wait for historians and history to deal with it properly. Was such a court and everything about it—from the time it took and its vast expense to the selectivity it displayed in who it indicted—the appropriate response to what had happened in 1994? Did it achieve what needed to be achieved? What was implied about the relationship between Africa and its people and the rest of the world, especially the "official" rest of the world, as represented by the United Nations and the international judiciary? If the court needed an eloquent argument, it was made by Richard Goldstone, the South African jurist who was the first chief prosecutor for the Yugoslav war crimes tribunal in The Hague. After horrid, unfathomable events, he proposed, there needed to be individual indictments. It must be seen that culpable individuals and not a whole people were behind such evils as war crimes and genocides. Others didn't get so lofty. Many saw the establishment of the tribunal as a grand (though necessary) public relations gesture. The ICTR had been "created out of shame," wrote *Boston Globe* journalist Elizabeth Neuffer. It had to be set up in order "to avoid charges of rank racism and ethnocentrism," observed Harvard law professor Martha Minow. "The UN had to be seen to be putting black African lives on the same footing as white European lives," stated Tanzanian-born Makau Mutua, a professor of law and director of the Human Rights Center at the State University of New York in Buffalo.[1]

Interestingly, despite Goldstone's resolute commitment to find ways to put blame squarely on the shoulders of human malefactors, the titles of two important books about Rwanda, including the one by General Dallaire, seemed to grope out beyond ordinary mortals to find their explanations. Everything was too horrible to remain within the realm of banal human behaviour; it could be elucidated only by plumbing the supernatural. A book that came out quickly from journalist Hugh McCullum, who made a dozen trips in and out of Rwanda in 1994 while the carnage was going on, literally while the blood of Rwandans was still soaking into the ground, was called *The Angels Have Left Us*,[2] using a quote the author had heard from a sixteen-year-old girl standing in an empty churchyard. Roméo Dallaire's memoir, penned a decade later after years during which he struggled with a huge burden of remorse and depression for his failure to prevent the catastrophe, was titled *Shake Hands with the Devil*.[3] Both these titles, much as the Greeks might have done, deferred to the gods in their attempts to tell the story of the awful things that had happened. Which was not to deny Goldstone's assertion that all the bad things had been the results of human actions. But who were those humans? What motivated them? Where could and should the fingers be pointed? What really was the purpose of the trials?

On one level, there was no doubt the ICTR was going to be a show trial. How could it not be? What happened in Rwanda in 1994 had shamed the world terribly. The United Nations and in particular the permanent members of the Security Council, countries like the United States, Britain, and France, were shocked in the aftermath of their failure and the world's very public dismay about their failure. On top of that, in 1994 the UN official in charge of peacekeeping, the official who as much as anyone had let down General Dallaire in his urgent requests for beefed-up support, was a near-to-the-top bureaucrat named Kofi Annan. The world community had some making up to do. What better way than a public trial?

Meanwhile, by 2004 in Rwanda itself, very different things were going on. The Tutsi-dominated government was solidly in place. When elections were held, Paul Kagame was confirmed in power with a plurality of 95%, despite the fact that opposing candidates were running against him; only Saddam Hussein or Slobodan Milosevic used to get those kinds of numbers. The Rwandan army was up to its neck in the troubles of its neighbour, the eastern Congo, where a reported three million people had died and millions more had become displaced in what was being called a civil war, but was actually a kind of general chaos, with a constant barrage of outsider incursions coming substantially from Uganda but also from Rwanda. And in its domestic jails, thousands—some reports said 80,000 people—now ten years older, languished, having been incarcerated for their actions during the genocide and still awaiting some sort of local disposition. Reports came out that something called "*gacaca* courts" were in the offing for those persons and perhaps as many as a million others. "*Gacaca*" means "grass," and refers to a traditional rural conflict-resolution system where families engaged in disputes with one another would gather on a patch of grass to work things out. The 'truth and reconciliation' commissions of post-apartheid South Africa were to be a model and, focusing on confession and apology, the *gacaca* courts were to ease the way to some form of healing and a national reconciliation.

The contrast could strike one only as phantasmagorical. The United Nations was spending hundreds of millions of dollars and more than a decade of its time to go after seventy malefactors while Rwanda claimed it had no resources whatsoever to deal with a thousand times that many who were accused, in large part, of the same bad deeds. Which raised another intriguing question. How were the choices made to send an accused into one camp as opposed to the other? How did the pastor and the doctor end up in Arusha instead of in the jails and courts back in Rwanda? Why were the 80,000 or million in Rwandan jails and *gacaca* processes there and not in Arusha? What was the difference? What made someone eligible for indictment by the UN?

The overt and publicly touted theory was that the UN would deal with the leaders, while leaving the domestic process to handle the followers. On the premise that what had happened in Rwanda was an orchestrated massacre, the UN would go after the ringleaders, those who, though they possibly had not committed the worst hands-on atrocities, were seen to be behind the planning and the encouragement—those in positions of leadership who had abdicated their responsibility to lead sanely and had permitted things to get out of control. On this basis, the net of the ICTR had snatched army generals, police leaders, the Anglican archbishop, a leader of the Interhamwe, and politicians, including, to the great glee of the prosecutors, a former prime minister.[4] These were to be held accountable and made an example of.

But this did not quite explain the Ntakirutimanas. Nothing had shown them to be anything close to leaders on any national scale. The two, father and son, enjoyed some social status because of their professional positions, but it was completely local. The defense, therefore, had another theory about their arrest and indictment. Local jealousies had conspired to denounce the pastor and the doctor to the UN prosecutors, which was enough to get them indicted. In short, it could well have been a frame-up—the system left itself open to that. Phil Taylor was sure "somebody wanted to take this family out, and we think we know who it was." In his journeys through Rwanda, Philip Gourevitch had tracked down two hospital orderlies who, in slightly conflicting accounts, fingered the pastor and his son. But the indictment itself was reputed to have come after children of the fellow pastors Ntakirutimana had failed to save had successfully approached the prosecutors. The leader of this group, according to Taylor, was a Seventh Day Adventist preacher's son and well-connected RPF politician named Assiel Kabera, who had been promptly appointed to replace the Hutu power as prefect for the district surrounding Mugonero. Now, alas, he was dead, having fallen out with the RPF and gotten himself assassinated. But it all fit with a theory Taylor clung to adamantly. Just as in 1994 Hutus were accused of getting rid of Tutsis, now in the aftermath the opposite was occurring, using all means possible, including this international court. The charges brought against their clients were part of a strategy, region by region, Taylor believed, to get the Hutu middle class, people like the Ntakirutimanas, out of the way. David Jacobs identified another culprit: the book itself by Philip Gourevitch with the searing title. "*We Wish to Inform You That Tomorrow We Will Be Killed with Our Families* was a seminal book," he stated. "I doubt that without it having been published there would have been an indictment."

Such attitudes and the suspicions they kept warm went to the heart of a great deal that made the Rwanda Tribunal and trials troublesome. The lawyers, in this case at least, persisted in their belief, stubbornly and sincerely held, that their clients had not done the deeds of which they were convicted, yet they were not surprised by the convictions. This was a court that hardly ever did otherwise. The widely held view was that the mere fact you were before the court meant you must have done something. An indictment seemed to be (almost) as good as a conviction. But if Taylor's research and viewpoint were correct, that a denunciation was all it took to secure an indictment, then anybody could be set up or framed. The system could be perverted, and unscrupulous or bitter persons could make use of the UN court as the unwitting tool to settle their local and private or family vendettas. The strategy to get the Hutu middle class out of the way, he suggested, would have no difficulty in achieving success.

Views as sour as these weren't helped by the processes through which the convictions were reached. The lawyers complained bitterly about the quality of evidence that was allowed against their clients. Had he been defending in a Canadian, American, or British court, David Jacobs noted bluntly, huge amounts of what was said against his clients would have been disallowed as hearsay, second hand, unsubstantiated, or not able to be substantiated. Ten years had passed, important witnesses no longer existed or could not be found; memories had faded, mythologies and legends had supplanted them. But instead of these factors becoming problems for the prosecution, they became problems for the defense. Prosecution witnesses who became confused on the stand were regularly given the benefit of the doubt. The prosecution was cut all kinds of slack, inevitably, in Jacobs's view, at the expense of the defense. And even if the prosecutors on occasion might be downright incompetent, the judges, as chief prosecutor del Ponte herself had pointed out, would step in to save the day. Adhering to the inquisitorial method common to the European system of justice, they acted more like agents of prosecution than the disinterested referees demanding fairness and burden of proof to be found presiding over trials in the Common Law systems of Britain, the United States, Australia, and Canada. The entirety of the defense bar frequently expressed frustration if not despair: the evidence upon which their clients were convicted seemed to them 'iffy'; the witnesses against their clients were iffy. When they set to work on their appeal, Jacobs and Clark zeroed in on this. "Credibility of the prosecution witnesses will have to be our main thing," said Clark.

Phil Taylor then told a story about a prosecution witness who did not mention in his deposition to the investigator that his wife and child had been killed. Yet, when he was on the witness stand, it came out, to the surprise of the defense, that they were not only killed, but purportedly shot by the pastor. Then the witness changed his mind and said it was by Gerard. But the problem, as any police department can tell you, was basic: "We have no forensic evidence," declared Taylor. "No bodies. We don't even know that these people were actually killed at all."

On top of it all, the court itself had shrunk in its mandate and original outlook, and, by so doing, had become vulnerable to charges of succumbing to political pressure. The tribunal had been set up in Arusha outside the borders of Rwanda itself originally for a very good reason. It had been assumed the tribunal would lay charges against both sides in the conflict, since both sides had committed terrible acts. That didn't happen. In the end it prosecuted only the losers, it was only the Hutu who came to Arusha. At one point, del Ponte did venture to bring indictments against members of the RPF (Rwandan Patriotic Front) now in power in Rwanda but that, interestingly, became the point at which she was also relieved of her job. She ceased being head of prosecution for the Rwanda Tribunal in 2003, though she kept her job with the Yugoslav Tribunal in The Hague; the indictments she had prepared against Tutsi members of the governing RPF remained sealed. The perception abruptly became that the UN trials were being run from Kigali, the Rwandan capital, that the government there was fingering those persons they wanted to be charged, and then was supplying the witnesses. The government of Paul Kagame, it was said, was pulling the strings of the UN trial as part of a strategy to keep their leading domestic enemies tied up for as long as possible. David Jacobs fumed that there were 'serial witnesses' who appeared in case after case—and often couldn't keep their stories straight. "The Rwandan government," he charged, "feeds the prosecution with information and witnesses."

Such doubts, though starting to stir among a skeptical minority, did not make a dent, at least not immediately, in the conventional wisdom. Rwanda was a genocide meticulously and brutally planned by Hutu extremists; the world community failed in first response but was making up for that. Correct society saved its worst possible insult for the doubters, fixing them with the label of "genocide deniers." However, the more time went by, the more such black and white definitions seemed just a little too pat, too convenient. With wear, they began to fray ever so slightly.

It took almost a decade, but in a prediction of how history might eventually see things, a nascent group of academics started to raise a critique. This went after the global party line and then the tribunal itself, challenging its assumptions as well as its practical achievements. "The ICTR is indistinguishable from victor's justice," wrote Alexander Zahar and Susan Rohol in early 2005 in the journal, *Genocide at the Millennium*.[5]

On the one side are the accusing members or sympathizers of the rebel-installed dictatorship that has ruled Rwanda since July 1994. On the other, in the dock, are members or sympathizers of the defeated regime. Witnesses testifying in defense of the latter are Rwandan nationals now living in exile. The accused persons' largest support group is still resident in Rwanda but its members are too terrified to testify in any accused's defense and there is evidence that in any event the Rwandan government would not allow potential defense witnesses to travel to the ICTR to testify.[6]

Disaffected Hutus, like Maurice Nsabimana, stuck now in exile in Brussels when he was not helping Ramsey Clark with the trial, were hugely encouraged by such bluntly put opinions. It meant that in their struggle to place an alternate interpretation on the events in their country, they were no longer out in left field all by themselves. The small but growing group of academics and yet-to-come historians dared to posit what had previously been the unthinkable: they were challenging even the sacred theory of the 'genocide'. The conventional wisdom was found to be "simplistic," wrote Zahar and Rohol. "This is because [it] reduces national defense to criminal conspiracy, political disagreement to tribal tension, and low tech civil war involving regular and irregular forces to genocide…. For most observers, the ICTR is a black box into which are poured witnesses (and close to $100 million per year), and from which periodically emerge judgments. For those who work inside the box, the production of judgments is all-important." They pointed to a kind of hypocrisy that confused the entire process, declaring that "at another level, the ICTR is a political instrument, or pawn, which also embodies high-minded rhetoric and genuine aspirations," which unfortunately at the end of the day meant only "prosecutions and judgments" compromised by "sentimentalism and politics."[7]

This was a harsh judgment, but certainly not a singular or isolated one. And some of those those sharing it had been in the very front line and on the ground during the battle: the defense attorneys. One needs to note that the main job of the defense is not simply to get one's client acquitted, but to make sure that even if they are guilty, all rights and protections—judicial, constitutional, due process, whatever—have been afforded them. Everyone must be convinced that the process was as fair as it could possibly have been and that everything that transpired was understood by the community in common. One Canadian lawyer was left thoroughly disillusioned by his experiences. "When I started out," David Jacobs told me, "I thought the idea [of the international tribunal] was a good thing. Now I'm completely opposed to it. It's a good idea in the abstract, but once you get down to the real world, you find it's highly political. You pretend you've got something when what you've got in reality is political and dangerous."

When I left Arusha, it was not on the same kind of plane that had brought me there, but on a bus, a minibus heading north to Nairobi, six hours away. Ibrahim drove me to the square where drivers marshalled a number of these vans early on a Sunday morning and as soon as ours had accumulated fifteen passengers, we took off. We departed the shadow of Mount Meru and passed under heavy, leaden skies through dry country-side with a low horizon of thorn bush vegetation where the only people we saw were Masai herdsmen with their cattle. At the Kenyan border we waited for an hour in a no-man's-land between two fences while Masai women and girls with blankets and trinkets to sell brought their beseeching faces right up against our van windows, tapping plain-tively on the glass to get our attention. All this time I thought about the Ntakirutimanas. I had to acknowledge I was nowhere near neutral on the case. I wanted the judges to find them not guilty, somehow I wanted them to get off. It wasn't, I felt, just because I'd spent all my time with their lawyers and was thus predisposed in their favour. Nor was it simply because of the phone conversations I'd had over the months with Gloria, the pastor's daughter, now isolated in her exile in faraway Laredo, where she worked as a nurse and prayed fervently for her father and brother. It wasn't even the evidence; prosecution witnesses had rolled out horrific stories of all that had transpired over the critical days in question at the Mugonero hospital compound and in the chaos of people fleeing the community afterward. If you wanted to pin bad deeds on the pastor and the doctor, you could read the evidence in ways that would permit you to do so.

My discomfited feelings, I realized, had more to do with the trial and the court itself.

The Rwanda Tribunal had been set up ostensibly to search for truth. If you are going to send people off to spend the rest of their lives in prison, you must be careful to do the search. Surely you must also do that if you recognize that you are part of an early examination of what is going to become history. It was said that one of the great, perhaps unexpected, contributions of the tribunal was the mass of narrative gathered from the grand totality of witnesses who appeared before it to tell their tales. Somehow, it would all add up to an invaluable documentary of the horror. But, incredible as all this evidence and narrative was, it was a jigsaw puzzle; each piece giving a glimpse, but only a glimpse, and not any of them providing anything near the whole truth in its entirety. Two hundred and fifty years ago, the French philosopher and encyclopedist, Denis Diderot, put the problem of truth seeking in less than absolute terms: "You have the right to expect that I shall search for the truth," he averred, "but not that I should find it."

The Rwanda Tribunal, however, suffered from a lack of Diderot's humility plus a great deal more. The pall of a priori certainties hung over everything. This was the imposition of global (i.e. foreign) justice. The losers in the Rwandan conflict, but only a tiny representation of them, were convicted in order to be made an example of, which did little to solve anything real in Rwanda itself. All that was expiated was the global community's own guilt. The problem, of course, is that nobody has ever come up with a better or an alternative system to deal with Rwandan-style atrocities, wherever they might happen. But the system they had here was definitely problematic. The process, at too many of its stages, left the impression of being heavy-handed, arbitrary, even absurd. Even the assumption of orchestrated genocide, so important in the structures of the initial analyses, might in the end have been more a distraction than a help. "What's interesting about all these cases," David Jacobs said, summing up all the trials that had transpired thus far in front of the tribunals, "is that they have not been able to put together evidence of the planned genocide. Everybody who has been convicted of anything has been convicted on the basis of eye-witness accounts of their behaviour but not of their creating any plan. The world in its view has stubbornly followed its own interpretation: "'We knew a genocide was going on, so that is genocide'," he said. What the tribunal had done without a doubt, though, was serve the needs of global public relations.

At the end of the day, the pastor and the doctor went off to jail, still protesting their innocence. In December 2004, their appeal was dealt with. After another look at the evidence and the judgments, the UN Appeals Chamber jurists meeting in The Hague, not Arusha, threw the original verdicts topsy turvy, yet with no real altering of the result. The conviction of the pastor in one of the events he was supposed to have been involved in was quashed, but the Appeal Chamber upheld the conviction for his activities at another event. His sentence remained ten years.[8] As for the doctor, the appeal court quashed two of three of his murder convictions but upheld the third, and upheld a conviction of aiding and abetting extermination.

13

WHO GOES TO AFRICA?

*M*Y PHONE RINGS IN TORONTO. It is my niece, a university student enrolled in science and health care, calling with exciting news. She has just been accepted to travel with a group of other young students, most of them from universities in the eastern United States, to the southern African country of Malawi. A small country, dreadfully poor, with a reputedly horribly backward government. "Great," I say, responding to her enthusiasm about being accepted for the trip, "what will you be doing?"

"Providing AIDS awareness to children and giving advice on forestation," she says.

I pause. Okay. It's hard to fault the good intentions of young people willing to surrender their summer holidays and pay all their own expenses to undertake such a mission. But the announcement given with such conviction unsettles me and leads me to another thought, or, more precisely, a question. I can imagine the lengthy journey on the airplane, all these fresh young people with their T-shirts probably printed with a logo of the service they are representing. I can picture the four-wheel-drive vehicles picking them up upon arrival to whisk them over terrible roads to outlying country villages. I imagine them struggling in a good-natured manner with a few words of tribal language and revelling in the gleeful response of the youngsters they will encounter and work with. I can see the brochures and, perhaps, the film strips they will show in any spot·fortunate enough to provide the electricity to run their projectors. The selflessness and pure good will of the young people, and no doubt those who had organized their venture, is heartwarming. But my question is this: how, I wonder, would a group of young African students from Malawi or some other country be received should they land in New Jersey or North Carolina or Canada for a six-week episode of giving advice to us?

This is not likely to happen; the relationship between Africa and the West, North America, and Europe is a one-way street. Africa has become necessary to our altruistic impulses, valuable as a place that is safe for us to help. I don't want, in any sense, to dismiss the help that is offered or the urge to be helpful, but it is hard not to be struck, even perplexed, by the automatic, almost axiomatic manner in which Africa has become the receptacle.

Again my phone rings. This time it is a woman, a stranger but someone who has seen the film about the scientific research being done with the sex workers of Pumwani and is planning a trip herself to Kenya. How, she wonders, might she, once she gets there, get in touch with Hawa? She wants to meet her and give her some money.

Africa has always existed for the outsider primarily—and one might argue most successfully—in our imagination. It is a real continent, but it both begins and most often ends in the realm of the imagination. We visit as tourists seeking the romance of the sight of a big animal, or as scientists looking for everything from the beginning of man to the keys to unlock deadly viruses, or as missionaries (now including in the very broadest sense those thousands who work in foreign aid, what are commonly called the NGOs) wanting to help and to change. When we make our appearance there, we do so painfully aware that we are balancing along a tightrope, both fascinated and frightened. That dichotomy, of course, is a large part of the attraction, we go in search of the perfect, enchanting scenery and the perfectly exotic experience while likewise believing the continent to be chillingly dangerous—though now it is not the wild animals and jungles that disturb us so much as the political and social and human dangers of a place we believe to be perpetually falling apart, havoc ready to erupt at any moment and certainly in more than one place at once: Rwanda, Sudan, Congo, Liberia. AIDS everywhere. But that is good; the more dangerous, the better.

Africa, by this token, has always been fair game. For Livingstone and Schweitzer to undertake their medical missionary work; for Burton and Speke, Stanley and a host of others to explore; for Leopold and Rhodes to plunder its natural wealth; for Conrad to find its—or his own—heart of darkness. The danger, the hazard, the potential for hardship has been the fuel in our tank. Most anybody in the West would give their eye-teeth for a session somewhere in Africa. I open my e-mail to find a message forwarded from the sister of a friend, a veterinarian momentarily part of a multi-disciplinary group of North Americans on a six-week visit to villages in rural Kenya. There they are studying pigs and human epilepsy. It is considered that I will appreciate the story of her adventures, and I do, the e-mail account is replete with tales of the hardships of the junket, the mosquitoes, the rugged roads. Yet, barely masked by the veneer of weary complaint is the bright light of unmistakable glee about what a lark this all is. And why would it not be? If you are a forty-five-year-old North American, what could be better than getting to travel around Kenya for six weeks in your own Land Rover? You are the recipient of the gift of a stupendous adventure, completely free from any possible accusation—from yourself or others—of indulgence; all can be justified by the argument that you are embarked on such earnest and such serious good.

A few peripheral things have changed since the days of Livingstone: the outsider is hardly ever now characterized as an explorer, missionary, settler etc. It is, in fact, very important *not* to be any of those old-fashioned things. The word we like to use now is "partner." The outsider attaches to an enterprise or cause that has some modicum of African interest at heart and African locals affiliated with it, and then defines him- or herself as a "partner." This choice of language, though it may or may not accurately reflect the nature of the relationships, doubtless reflects the depth of the desire to reconstitute the parameters of the relationships. Rather than a plunderer, you now can be some kind of visiting consultant. Yet, the essential interplay between the foreign outsider and the local person or people in whatever African country remains not that much altered: the assumptions behind the engagement, the inequality of the power relationship, look strikingly very much as they have always looked. The defining emblem now, though, is not the pith helmet but the four-wheel-drive vehicle, almost always white.

Among those travelling most easily now into Africa (even the terminology "into" is quite peculiar to Africa; we would not likely say we were going "into" Europe), one group that does it almost seamlessly are research scientists. My veterinarian friend would fit in this category as perhaps would even my niece and her colleagues, though they were all undergraduate students. In the grand scheme of things, scientists have achieved a unique position, having not only replaced but superseded the missionary and the explorer of former days. By searching for answers, the researcher has become an explorer permitted to look into every corner and to trek to the furthest reaches; armed with insight into mysteries, he or she becomes the missionary looked up to for answers and explanations of the otherwise unfathomable. Equipped with credible expertise and provided authority by their attention to the immensity of the problems that cry out for solution—particularly in human health—their way is paved to go wherever they want, no border can stop them. AIDS, in particular, has turned much of at least sub-Saharan Africa into a gigantic laboratory, but all kinds of research, such as the quest regarding epilepsy and pigs, readily gets a green light and foreign funding. When I commented about the esoteric nature of so many of the foreign-based research projects I observed in Kenya, one North American scientist only laughed. "There is no corner," he retorted, "that we will leave unswabbed."

Trained scientists are, by necessity, unsentimental, pragmatic, clear-headed, and Cartesian. Yet, if you are a Western scientist presuming to do your research in Africa, those attributes are only the beginning of what you will need to negotiate the pitfalls lining the periphery of your journey. What research scientists face, along with the riddles of microbes and viruses, are the problems like the kinds of co-dependence that inevitably get built into the structure of their engagement, however short or long it may be. To do this, they have to remember that all assumptions must be periodically put up for re-evaluation. They are obliged to work out with their hosts the (not small) matter of the reciprocity of relationships, understanding that the question of values can frequently turn into an enormous stumbling block. The perpetuating problem of values is not so much necessarily that outsiders impose their own as it is that we feel so free to reinterpret those of our hosts.

On top of it all, research scientists must be consciously aware of their motivations if only because, like the missionaries and explorers before them, one might assume their motivations to be faultlessly self-evident. In point of fact, they never are.

I return to my overexcited niece. "Your trip is going to be a great experience," I tell her, "but you might want to remember one thing."

"What's that?" she asks. I can tell the tone in my voice has made her apprehensive.

"You're going to receive more while you're there than you're ever going to give; you're going to learn a great deal more than you're ever going to teach."

KISUMU,
KENYA
2004

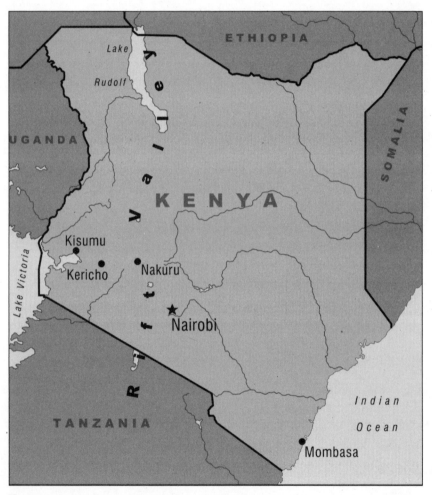

KENYA

14

THE NYANZA CLUB

*K*ENYA AIRWAY'S EVENING FLIGHT from Nairobi banked into the final phase of its steep descent. Pressing my face to the porthole window, I looked down at a swirl of blue-green waters: Lake Victoria, the second largest freshwater lake in the world; the fabled environment of King Rumanika and explorers Burton and Speke. The lake circumnavigated in a canoe by Henry Morton Stanley looking to see if any part of it emptied out to become the Nile. Then, all of a sudden, we were past the water and it was all palm trees and elephant grass as the little plane levelled in toward the runway delivering, at precisely 7:00 p.m., its twenty passengers to the small Kisumu airport. Minutes later, waiting on the damp tarmac for the luggage to be brought round on the wire-sided wagon pushed by the baggage handlers, I looked about to see if there might be a taxi. Almost instantly a smiling young man approached. He asked if I needed a ride, then led me to where a fleet of sagging cars, none of them with taxi markings, was parked. Each had a staff of two, the driver and the tout. Mine introduced himself, "Moses," and his partner, "Johnson." Moses Onyango and Ochanga Johnson, with me in the back seat, set off for the ten-minute trip to town. It had rained, leaving puddles in the road and everything a verdant green.

In the gathering dusk, cows grazed in the ditches and we passed people on bicycles.

"Are you with an NGO?" Moses turned in his seat and posed what was probably the inevitable question for the newly arrived white person.

"No," I answered, "but I'm visiting one. UNIM." I provided the acronym for a project set up two years earlier to carry out a scientific study by the universities of Nairobi, Illinois, and Manitoba. I was slightly hesitant, I wondered whether UNIM might not be a bit controversial locally. The idea behind it was to test an hypothesis that circumcision of young males would affect HIV rates—for the better—and, to do that, persuading a great number of young Kisumu men, men like Moses and Johnson, to get circumcised. "Do you know them?" I asked.

"Oh yes," Moses answered. "We know Bob, we know Kawango. Sometimes we drive them."

They drove me to a place called the Nyanza Club, then deposited me at the front gate and helped with my bag. "You'll want to go to the clinic tomorrow," Moses stated. "What time will we pick you up?"

In my mind I had settled on an alternate plan for getting to the clinic where the project was being studied, which was about four kilometres away on the other side of town. On a previous visit I'd worked out what I considered a perfect local transportation strategy: a fairly agreeable walk past government buildings and park-like gardens for the first part of the trip until I reached the edge of downtown. Then all I had to do was flag down a bicycle taxi, locally called *boda-boda,* climb on the extended seat behind the cyclist, and get the rest of the trip for a cost of about twenty-five cents. I was intending to do that now rather than shell out seven to ten dollars for the car taxi. Yet I could hardly refuse these friendly fellows. "All right," I agreed, "pick me up at nine." I gave Johnson a business card so he would remember my name.

The Nyanza Club is where all visitors to UNIM are billeted. I'd been there before, two years earlier. My first impression was that the place had seen better days: a broken board in the floor of the dining room complained loudly; burned-out bulbs left the room gloomy while wiring in need of an upgrade caused what illumination there was to flicker ominously—which might, in fact, have done service to the food, but that's another matter. The place seemed sad, badly in need of paint, crying out for someone to replace the faded curtains printed with Bambi deer that covered the windows. Things were not much better in the bar and lounge next door and, across the parking lot in the guest quarters, where people like me can arrange to stay for days or weeks while we are in town, the towels and bathmats had faded 50% since my last visit, just as the stains in the tub had deepened.

Yet, the place had its magic. From the verandas of the guest rooms, I could look out past palm trees and papyrus stands to the shimmering waters of the lake stretching to the horizon. Black ibis and fish eagles circled above while, in the distance, the Uganda ferry could be spotted leaving the harbour for its daily chug to Kampala. There were kingfishers and red-chested cuckoos in the surrounding marshes and, at night, after you tumbled down your mosquito netting, all the sounds were soothing: the croak of frogs, the whirring wings of bats taking off from under the eaves to chase dragonflies, the swish of the night guard's rubber boots.

The old British aren't running the Nyanza Club any longer. A study of the plaques on the wall in the lounge, listing directors and secretaries, shows exactly when the colonials who comprised the Kenya Railways elite gave way to what is now the local Indian bourgeoisie. All the Scottish names—Horne and Wilson and McTough—abruptly turn into Awori and Basheer-ud-Deen. Nothing, apparently, changed for the black Africans who remained as they were: chambermaids, waiters, tennis coaches, night guards or *askaris*, and little boys who retrieved the tennis balls on the red clay courts. But the evening and weekend clientele now whiling away languid hours inside the lounge or sitting at the tippy metal tables by the pool had become largely Indian. Women wrapped in saris eyeballed their bored teenaged sons and daughters; the parents, dressed carefully, exuded a self-conscious formality while the children appeared to harbour no wish so great as to find a working television and tune in MTV from Mumbai.

That was the local clientele. The other guests were visiting North Americans, most of them scientists, or hangers-on like me. "Where is your friend Ian?" asked Hezbone, the maitre d', the next morning when I settled in for breakfast. He was referring to Ian Maclean, a Canadian from Winnipeg who had been coming at least twice a year to oversee the functioning of the equipment at the UNIM lab. Arriving tomorrow, I told him. Maclean was held in reverential awe by Hezbone, in large part because Ian was generous to a fault, having once shipped a gas barbeque all the way from Canada and donated it to the kitchen. When he arrived this time, he would bring with him his own maple syrup for pancakes and Hezbone would cart out the French press coffeepot that waited specially for him in the dining-room cupboard.

Ian and people like him had become an important and sought-after cog in the local economy. Scientific investigation, practised for the most part by visiting foreigners, had reached the status of an industry in Kisumu—HIV researchers, malaria researchers, all kinds of researchers. And it wasn't just Kisumu. In the last years of the twentieth century and the early years of the twenty-first, great swathes of Africa had become rich territory for research scientists. AIDS science, in particular, had turned much of at least sub-Saharan Africa into a gigantic laboratory. One could only make a guess at how many projects or researchers might be operating at any given moment; the number changed daily. I was told maybe fifty projects were going on in Kenya, maybe a hundred. Some projects were long-term, some lasted only a few days. But as a phenomenon, it was of stupendous import. Countries such as South Africa, Botswana, Uganda, and certainly Kenya witnessed the arrival of new foreign scientists as an almost constant stream. For the researchers, it was like a gold rush; if you had a plausible project, especially regarding AIDS, North American or European universities and funding bodies were keen to finance you. It could be heady stuff. Projects became more and more specific, more and more esoteric.

On the other side of things, the African hosts appeared ready to embrace the researchers and their projects with gusto, not least for economic reasons. That the fruits of these investigations might hold positive possibilities for the people of Kenya seemed almost incidental to the fact of their impor-tance to the economy, both national and local. Certainly the presence of the scientists was important to the economy of the Nyanza Club.

Scientists, both as individuals and as a class, I'd come to understand as odd sorts, though I mean this in as generous a way as possible; obsessed by minutiae, each with his or her own specialty and field of research, which then became integral to their identity. These specialties caused fellow scientists to refer to one another as 'malaria people', 'HIV people', 'water study people', 'cholera people'. At the Nyanza Club the last time round, I had been breakfasting with Bob Bailey, one of the UNIM researchers taxi driver Moses had spoken of during our ride, when an attractive woman, newly arrived, came over to our table to introduce herself. Bailey reached out to shake her nicely manicured hand and asked, "Are you a diarrhea person?" Scientists, I'd also discovered, could be intensely clubby, especially when they were away from home and out on their field projects. They arrived in Kisumu in small troops and then made sure to stick together. Even in the breakfast room of the Nyanza Club, each group jealously staked its turf, offering careful, measured greetings as others showed up. One table of newly arrived visitors was from Washington, overseer or bureaucratic types from the National Institutes of Health garbed accordingly in suits made only slightly more casual for the tropics. Another table would soon be commandeered by the HIV researchers I was there to visit. The largest group at the moment, requiring three tables, was entomologists from Michigan State University undertaking a six-week-long malaria study. These were real in-the-field scientists dressed for the part in blue jeans and rubber boots, their outfits at the end of the day completely sweat-stained. Their work was intricate and intense. Word went round that they were making videotapes of mosquitoes copulating and had turned the balcony of one of their rooms into a sound stage.

At nine o'clock, with the sun already becoming hot, I walked up to the front gate to wait for my promised taxi. It didn't come. I asked the guard if he knew Johnson and Moses and had they been round. "Not yet," he said. I decided to give them five minutes. It was Saturday, the clinic would be open only for the morning and then closed until Monday, I didn't want to waste the precious hours. After five minutes, I set off on foot, muttering a few complaints about the unreliability of a couple of drivers from whom I expected better; my old plan would have to be activated after all. But then I calmed down. Under the shade of the great trees that spread across the road, the walk was pleasant. I passed the inevitable grazing cows and the whitewashed walls fronting provincial government build-ings. The Kenyan flag flapped dutifully in the breeze. Two workers with machetes were cutting grass on the boulevard, chopping away rhythmically with steady, arching swings. Using my passing as an excuse, they took a break and waved. Suddenly, a banged-up grey Peugeot pulled up beside me. I didn't recognize the driver, who held up a small white card. "Is this you, Mr Larry?" he asked. It was my business card. "Johnson and Moses are very sorry," he said. "Their car has broken down and it will take until afternoon to repair it. They have sent me to find you."

The UNIM clinic was situated in a compound that was on the verge of achieving a sort of critical mass in terms of health care activities. Next door was a municipal clinic, newly fixed up, where, on this morning, city food workers were lined up for their monthly cholera tests. At the end of the parking lot, new construction was underway on two more buildings that would join the municipal clinic and UNIM with their own undertakings, both in the fields of HIV research. The UNIM clinic was smart and stylish, nicely designed, of gleaming white stucco with the clinic logo painted in bright blue. Across the fence, a private girls' school looked decidedly shabby by comparison. Constructed in 2001, the clinic had been doubled in size by an addition in 2002. Inside, the spacious waiting room was filled already that morning with about twenty-five young men. In one direction were consulting rooms and the surgery; in the other, a file storage room and a fully operational lab. Upstairs were offices, a conference room, and a data processing centre. I asked for Kawango, the other person mentioned by Moses on the taxi ride the night before, and was directed to an office next to the lab. A tall, cheerful woman wearing an African print costume and sporting horn-rimmed glasses greeted me.

Dr Kawango Agot was a Kisumu local. She had left Kenya as a young woman to study in America and came back with a PhD in medical geog-raphy from the University of Washington. For her thesis, she'd returned to her roots and done something that turned out to help immensely in her interview for this job: she'd undertaken a study of circumcision in the Kisumu area. On her desk was a well-thumbed bible and a cell phone, which, when it rang, burbled "Waltzing Mathilda." As clinic manager, she was in charge of hiring all the local staff, more than forty of them, including the surgeons who performed the circumcisions on through to counsellors, lab staff, recruiters, drivers, data-entry people, cleaners, and security guards. One of these security guards, a Samburu tribesman named Retunoi Lesiago, Kawango got a great kick out of telling me, had had to sign his clinic contract with a thumbprint. But in the intervening two years of employment, he'd learned to print his name.

The infrastructure under Kawango's control was all to support a single venture, a clinical study that, after almost three years, had arrived at its halfway point. They were facing, she told me, two challenges: keeping track of the clients they'd already enrolled, 1700 at this point; and recruiting 1000 more young men they still needed to fulfill their mission. "We are doing pretty well on the first," she said. A major component of any clinical study is follow-up. In this case, everybody they'd enrolled was supposed to return for regular medical checkups and HIV tests, and to provide the researchers with up-to-date lifestyle information. They were batting about 90%, having, Kawango admitted, lost track of about 10% of their clients. But then she brightened. This was less than the 15% they had anticipated. From time to time, they'd had to send trackers a full day's journey to Nairobi or Mombasa to find a client they needed to talk to, but the inconvenience didn't seem to her extraordinary. "Most of our participants are jobless," she shrugged, "so we can't expect them to stay around; if they see an opportunity, they leave."

On the second task of recruiting the 1000 young men they still needed, she nodded toward the twenty-five sloping bodies outside her door. One by one, Kawango believed, they would achieve their number.

On Monday morning, Bob Bailey picked me up in the project van. Bailey, whom I'd first met two years earlier, was freshly returned from a visit back to Chicago and had brought his family, wife and two sons, to Kisumu for a sabbatical year, settling them into a house on the nice side of town, not far from the Nyanza Club. That morning he had a problem to solve that was typical of his life here and a great deal different from the sorts of things he'd be doing in his classroom back in Illinois. A week earlier a rainstorm and accompanying power surge had fried his laptop computer and we needed to fetch it from the repair shop. The Indian-run shop was on the second floor of a dusty building that otherwise purveyed animal feed and over-stuffed furniture, the kinds of sofas that really dominate a room. We climbed the stairs to be greeted by the proprietor, a young man in a gleaming white shirt who shook hands with Bailey while proudly explaining that he had been able to save his files. He commenced opening various of them to demonstrate. "Oh god," exclaimed Bailey in mock horror. "Don't look at the pictures, they're all penises."

Bailey, born in New York, began his career not as a medical scientist but as an anthropologist. He earned his PhD (and published a *National Geographic* photo story) in 1989 studying pygmies in what was then Zaire. It would be a stretch, almost comic, to imagine the 6'2" beanpole researcher mingling with 4'8" pygmies, but he got hooked on the African continent and, after obtaining a Master's degree in epidemiology and public health, returned to Uganda and western Kenya to conduct surveys on attitudes and beliefs about male circumcision. Now he was co-researcher with a Canadian, Dr Stephen Moses, here.

With Bailey's once again functioning laptop under his arm, we returned to the clinic. Kawango greeted us by announcing that Ian Maclean had arrived and telling us to go straight to the lab to find him. A PhD in micro-biology, Maclean was the kind of guy someone might first mistake for a delivery person or handyman. His Presbyterian roots forbade his having a pretentious bone in his body. His standard uniform was blue jeans and a work shirt with the sleeves rolled up, and his motto seemed to be "lead by example." If any moving was to be done, nobody carried more boxes than he.

In the lab we found him examining one of the refrigerators. The same power surge that damaged Bailey's laptop computer had disabled the refrigerator. But it was not going to be catastrophic, Maclean announced, the problem could be solved locally. All he needed was to locate a new compressor. "Thank goodness it wasn't the -80 degree fridge," he told us, "because for that we'd have to ship in a whole new one." Having had the main responsibility for equipping it, Maclean knew the layout of this lab intimately. In November 2001 he had shipped all the equipment—which included freezers, centrifuge, and all manner of other assorted machinery—from Canada and then had flown over himself to set it up. In his luggage, he'd carried his own crowbar and tin snips to open the shipping crates. That year he worked through until Christmas, and then returned in early January for another six weeks.

That morning, new samples of blood serum, plasma, and urine arrived at a steady clip, to be sorted by the Kenyan staff, Walter Otiendo, Edith, and Lawrence. Surrounding them, along with the refrigerators, were tanks for shipping these specimens. The home labs for the researchers were eight time zones away, with those faraway headquarters serving both as source of supply and destination for product or samples. In Canada, several times a year, Maclean still organized a shipping container filled with whatever he thought the lab would need: rubber gloves, single-use scalpels, possibly a new refrigerator. The container would make its way from Winnipeg to Halifax by truck or train, then to Mombasa by sea, and then inland to Kisumu by truck. In the other direction, the blood serum, urine, and severed foreskins travelled by air. The amount of this specimen shipping was phenomenal. Maclean did the math for me: 2700 clients times six visits to the clinic. Such a volume was actually more, the researchers determined, than their science needed; halfway into the project they'd probably looked at enough foreskins back in Chicago to know everything they needed to know on that aspect of their study. Yet, they couldn't stop sending them without first getting permission from both their funders and the various ethics boards that controlled their research.

It is easy to forget how recent are the innovations that actually make all such specimen shipment possible. In 1927, Dr Fritz Trenz, a Swiss doctor/ missionary working in Gabon, West Africa, faced the puzzle of how to transport a vibrion of cholera bacteria to his laboratory at home in Strasbourg, France. He came to the conclusion he had no alternative but to drink a vial containing the bacteria. He knew what would happen but gulped it down anyway. On board ship, he predictably became deathly ill with fever and dysentery, but once back in France was able to extract a healthy specimen—from his own body. With freezing, refrigeration, and air transportation, transfer of specimens has come a long way since Fritz Trenz.

Still, the logistics of running a project in some far-off corner of Africa, from the uncertainties of electrical power surges to the complexities of shipping, are monumental. At mid-morning Maclean enquired if I wanted to come with him and Walter Otiendo, the lab manager, on a little visit. Stepping out of the clinic, we followed Albert, a newly arrived man in a Nehru shirt, across to one of the new buildings under construction, this one for a University of California researcher who was going to undertake a study on the confluences of HIV and herpes. In the new building, in rooms still smelling of fresh paint, Albert, who was the on-the-ground coordinator for the not-yet-arrived scientist, showed where the various offices would go. What he wanted to get mainly, though, was Ian's and Walter's opinion on the area that would function as a lab. Was it properly designed? Had they forgotten anything? They took a look at it. "Is the counter big enough for your centrifuge?" Maclean asked. Then he inquired how they planned to send their specimens back, in this case to San Francisco. Albert answered they would send them on dry ice, which prompted Maclean to raise doubts. "Dry ice can't make it all the way to North America reliably, you should go with liquid nitrogen," he said. "That way, even if your tank gets hung up somewhere for a couple of weeks, your samples will still be all right."

All sorts of technologies were working to keep projects like this functioning. And the researchers had come to rely on them implicitly. Before the invention of e-mail, Bob Bailey said, everybody would have had to live on-site to do what the UNIM consortium was doing. Now he could easily stay in touch with Kawango from his office or house back in Chicago, transferring not only daily messages but also data. Steve Moses, their other partner, was at that moment in India but remained likewise in daily contact, again through e-mail. Imagining a time before this was commonplace was almost like going back to the days when Dr Trenz was imbibing cocktails of cholera bacteria before boarding his ship home. Later, I found Maclean and Bailey huddled over the computer, examining another bit of novelty. On the screen, Ian had called up an image he had purchased from a satellite photo service, an aerial photo, blurry at first, of the town of Kisumu. Taken on an extraordinarily cloudless day, it showed the shores of Lake Victoria and the contours of the town. They were able to zoom in all the way to individual houses, including the one where Bailey, his wife, Nadine, and two sons, Alex and Nathan, were staying for the duration of their sabbatical. "I didn't know my neighbour had a pool," Bailey exclaimed. The image scrolled to the poorer part of town, a scramble of tin roofs where there were no street names and no house numbers. "We could print out sections of this," Ian proposed, "and the recruiters could go house to house while checking off on the map that they'd been there." Bailey agreed excitedly. Three years into their study, they had exhausted the bars and fishing docks around town and wanted now to go house to house to chase down their subjects. And they wanted to do it effectively and methodically. The technology of satellite imagery would help.

15

CIRCUMCISING AFRICA

O N TUESDAY MORNING, I WAS APPROACHED by one of the clinicians, Bernard Ayieko, who told me that if I wanted to watch a
procedure, I should come to the surgery in twenty minutes. I jumped at
the opportunity with only the tiniest misgiving: it was perhaps voyeuristic.
But I convinced myself that it was the journalistic thing to do and I'd never
get another chance quite like this. The surgery was a smallish room just
back of the waiting area and counsellors' offices. Ayieko, who was stocky,
wore round, steel-framed glasses, and was thirty-nine years old, was already
scrubbed and gowned, as was his assistant, George Odhiambo. On the table,
half under the green drape, lay a tall young man in his early twenties. Earlier,
although he certainly looked the part, Ayieko had stressed that he was not
a real doctor. He had been trained as a clinician to do only this one specific
surgery. He had perfected his skill when posted with the Family Planning Association of Kenya and then, when he took the job at UNIM, had
undergone, along with the two other surgeons, an intensive seminar from a
urologist flown in from America, from Seattle.

George handed me a mask and pointed to the corner where I had been
designated to stand, out of the way though still assured of a good view.

Through the window I could see burgundy-uniformed girls from the primary school next door well into their noisy recess. Attempting friendliness, I offered my hello to the lanky young man stretched out on the table and asked him his name. Immediately Ayieko cautioned me, "Because of the anonymity of the clinical trial, you can only refer to him by his number." He would have to remain Client 1665. Client 1665 grinned manically and rolled his eyes. His lower abdomen had been shaved, though he had not yet been administered anaesthetic. "He is very nervous," conceded George, breaking the soft Swahili patter he had been maintaining in an effort to put the young man at ease. Ayieko readied his long needle. Client 1665 jumped. George continued to talk soothingly, much as he might to a high-strung racehorse.

Bob Bailey first met Dr Stephen Moses, his co-researcher, in 1997 at a meeting at the Centers for Disease Control in Atlanta, Georgia. The two men shared a niggling preoccupation. Moses, fifty-two years old, was born in Toronto but for ten years, from the mid-1980s to 1996, lived in Nairobi, where he collaborated with another Canadian, Manitoba's Dr Frank Plummer. Almost immediately after meeting Bailey, he started musing about an idea he'd been thinking about for some time, the role of circumcision in HIV transmission. Bailey's ears perked up. Moses and Plummer, at that time, had already published scientific papers pointing out that probably due to better hygiene, African men who had been circumcised suffered fewer STDs of any sort. Plummer's research had also pointed out links between nasty STDs such as chancroid and gonorrhea and susceptibility to HIV, one of the theories being that the ulcers and sores that go with traditional STDs create portals for HIV entry. On top of this there were some, as then untested, theories about HIV receptor cells in foreskin tissue. To a man like Moses, with his public health bent, this was all enough to appear quite convincing. But it was theory only. What was missing was the definitive study, the clinical trial that would link circumcision and HIV prevention strongly enough to justify making circumcision part of the global anti-HIV strategy. And it would never happen, he lamented, unless a group could be brought together who would agree to be randomized, on the draw of a lottery, consent to be circumcised—or not—and allow researchers to observe what transpired. Which is where an idea that would cement the collaboration popped into Bailey's head. Recalling the surveys he'd made not long before in western Kenya, he piped up: "Maybe the Luo will."

Kenya is a country of thirty million people. But though it is a modern nation, it is also a tribal society. In the northwest corner, pressing up against Lake Victoria and the Ugandan border, two million strong, are the Luo. Of all the tribes in Kenya, the Luo fulfilled two conditions that made them appealing for such a study as Bailey and Moses wanted to carry out: they did not have a ritual of circumcision as part of their tradition, and they had the country's highest HIV infection rate. When Bailey and Moses were making their proposal, the HIV rate in Kenya was widely accepted as 14%. In Luoland, however, it was more than twice that.

The politics of getting their study approved had not been terribly difficult. Moses had his base in Nairobi while Bailey's anthropological surveys in Uganda and Kenya left him well-situated on the ground. He had gained the confidence of Dr Richard Muga, the provincial medical officer for the local Nyanza province and a force in Kenyan health care. He'd been assured, as well, that Luo elders, while not having circumcision as part of their tradition, did not actively oppose it. With Muga's blessing, Bailey and Moses approached Dr J.O. Ndinya-Achola, professor and former dean at the medical school at the University of Nairobi (and also a Luo), for an in-country partnership. They then applied for grants to the National Institutes of Health in the US and the Canadian Medical Research Council (later to become Canadian Institutes for Health Research), requesting five million dollars in total.

The subjects they decided on for the trial would be young men between eighteen and twenty-four. This was a highly vulnerable as well as volatile group. Eighteen-year-old men in Kisumu had an HIV infection rate of 4%, which, by the time they reached twenty-four, spiked to 25%. Bailey and Moses had been told there were a potential 38,000 young men in the Kisumu district fitting into their demographic. They wanted 2700 of them. To get into the study, each young man would have to test negative to HIV and be willing to be randomized—that is, agree to be circumcised right away if the lottery put him into that cohort or wait two years if he fell into the control group. Members of both groups had to agree to come back six times over a two-year period to continue to be tested and answer questions about their lifestyles and sexual habits. In return, they would receive some medical care and 300 shillings (about five dollars) for each visit to cover transportation expenses. In 2001, the first of the money was committed by Canada's Medical Research Council, and, with it, the two North American scientists commenced construction on their clinic and hired Dr. Kawango Agot. She, in turn, hired the rest of the staff, including Ayieko and George.

Ayieko and George performed as many as three circumcisions a day, and, by this point in the project's trajectory, had done literally hundreds of the operations. Each took about ninety minutes from the beginning of prep, the scrubbing and laying out of the instruments, until the patient finally got off the table and wobbled out the door. The actual operation itself took about forty minutes, though Ayieko, who liked to clock such things, said that the fastest one they had accomplished had been twenty-seven minutes. Usually the circumcision surgeries went smoothly, though not always. Three times, Ayieko confessed, his patients had bolted, right at the last moment when they were on the table, already shaved, and he himself was scrubbed, gloved, and gowned. "But that's okay," he said. "Some of them get scared, they're scared of the pain. So they have the right to leave."

Client 1665 might have been one of those who considered leaving but instead remained fast, lying tense on the table, staring wide-eyed at the ceiling when he wasn't rolling his head to look beseechingly over at me. "Talk to me," he said at one point, "so that I don't have to think about what is going on down there." Before both of us knew it, though, the snip had been made. "Here," said George, holding the severed foreskin in his tweezers in front of the young man's blinking face. "Never to see it again." The suturing complete and bandages applied, 1665 gingerly slid off the table, worked himself carefully back into his jeans, and thanked us by weakly shaking hands all round. "You know," Ayieko cautioned him, "you're not to ride your bicycle for at least three days." The young man nodded and limped from the room. Outside the window, the burgundy-uniformed schoolgirls were still at their play.

It would have been quite a journey to know everything that was going on inside the head of Client 1665, both at that moment and also in the days leading up to his submitting himself for his surgery. What had motivated him? What had convinced him to volunteer? Was he moved by self-interest? Was the promise of perpetual health care and the prospect of pocket change every time he came to the clinic all it took? Was he persuaded personally by the possibility that circumcision might be a form of prevention that could save his life (though all counselling given the clients stressed the point that the jury was still out, only their study *might* prove something)? Perhaps he was moved in some altruistic way by the larger argument put forward by the foreign researchers and their local staff that this was a vital experiment in the war against AIDS. Whatever his motivation, he had, after all, undergone an excruciating surgery, one that would take him out of commission in both work and play for some time, and one neither popularly accepted nor even recommended by the culture within which he had grown up and lived.

These sorts of questions were of acute interest to the scientists, as well, especially to Bailey, whose main hat, the one he couldn't seem to get rid of no matter how deeply he got enmeshed in medical science, was that of the anthropologist. There was more to medical research, he averred, than simply testing medical procedures; the whole life and history of a society or community were wrapped up in beliefs and practices that impinged on how the research that called itself 'science' would be viewed, accepted, cooperated with, and carried out.

From Bailey's standpoint, a study such as theirs necessitated an interaction with the community as a whole and included matters from public relations to intelligence gathering. One day he introduced me to a young man, Dipesh Pabari. Born in Kisumu, Pabari was a fourth-generation Asian (Indian) Kenyan with a Master's degree in anthropology from the University of London's School of Oriental and African Studies. He was twenty-six years old and in twenty years would look like the actor Ben Kingsley. Desiring to learn as much as they could about what the people of Kisumu thought of their enterprise, Bailey and Moses had hired Pabari to look at the perceptions of people in the community at large. The assignment was not only to accumulate and collate a record of those perceptions, but to try to discern how those might have gotten formed and how they were influenced by culture, both that of the local community and the traditional culture of the Luo. It was anthropology, psychology, and cultural studies rolled into one, and a project Pabari relished. The young man told me he was euphoric about his task. "I'm being paid to get to know my community," he told me. He was accomplishing his mission by getting on his bicycle every morning and scooting around Kisumu's bars and markets in order to talk and to listen.

From Pabari I learned the difference between a "whistle," in the jargon of young Kisumu men, an uncircumcised penis, and a "spear," one that is circumcised. I also learned something that he said had surprised the researchers. Circumcision was becoming increasingly popular throughout Kenya and, by not being circumcised, the Luo were, in fact, a bit on the outs —something that didn't sit well with the young. Among young people, there was developing, Pabari discovered, a strong desire to conform, to act and look like Kenya's other tribes. Even young Luo women were reportedly coming to prefer men with 'spears'. For Bailey and Moses, this information allayed one of their great fears, which was that they would have a problem recruiting. Initially, Pabari said, he encountered some negative opinion about the project, not to mention some weird rumours. A few people told him that circumcision was a form of devil worship, and others passed on hearsay that the clinic was collecting foreskins, drying them, and sending them to America to be made into handbags. But negative views turned out to be the exception. "Ninety-nine percent of the reaction," he insisted, "is favourable."

He faced one myth, however, broadly held enough that it ought, he said, to cause worry. With sufficient frequency to make him take note, people told him they believed getting tested was not simply how one found out one *had* AIDS, it was in fact the way one *caught* AIDS. "My cousin, my friend, my colleague," they would tell him, "went and got tested and now he has AIDS." The implication in their minds seemed to be that if he hadn't gone to the clinic for that test, he would still be fine. As a form of denial from uneducated people who dreaded bad news, this was perhaps understandable, but such a view held colossal consequences. Immediately, for the research project, it could cancel out the good news on the recruiting front; since the first thing required for one to enroll in the study was an HIV test, such an attitude could keep people away, especially those at the low end of society, the higher risk groups the scientists craved. In the broader picture, such a myth fed by misinformation could prove disastrous in the battling of an epidemic like AIDS.

On the issue of whether circumcising was okay, Pabari found that the project did not transgress any deeply held community belief. This caused Bailey and Moses to heave a sigh of relief. Opinion regarding circumcision appeared to be leaning toward the positive among the young. I got a deeper understanding of this when, back at the clinic, I sat down with Maurice Onyango, one of the counsellors assigned to deal with clients when they first came through the door. Onyango was a proud Luo and confirmed that some long-held traditions of the tribe were changing. A soft-spoken fellow in a green striped golf shirt, he himself personified the transition through which his tribe (indeed much of Kenyan society) was passing at the beginning of the twenty-first century. His father had three wives, and two siblings, the children of one of those wives, had gone through a traditional Luo coming-of-age rite called *Nago*, which involved removing the bottom four incisor teeth. But Onyango had all his teeth and only one wife. And while Luo tradition was not to circumcise, the taboo against it, he confirmed, agreeing with what Pabari had been finding, was not strong. Young men were embracing it, especially when they were told about hygiene and when they learned about the possibility of lower susceptibility to STDs.

Since *Nago* was no longer widely practised, Onyango said Luo boys were left without any real initiation ceremony. Which appeared to be fine with him. When Kenya's largest tribe, the Kikuyu, for example, had a ceremony for circumcision, "there is," he said, "a lot of pain." In Onyango's opinion, "most people prefer the hospital method." Onyango took me into a room where the follow-up questionnaires were kept. The system of documentation at the project was extensive and boxes of questionnaires waiting for dissemination were stacked to the ceiling. He pulled one and opened it. Clients on their second follow-up visit after surgery were to answer the following questions:

Are you satisfied or dissatisfied with the results of the circumcision?

If you have had sexual intercourse since your circumcision, did your sex partner express any opinion about your circumcision?

If yes, was your partner

1: very satisfied

2: somewhat satisfied

3: somewhat dissatisfied

4: very dissatisfied

Eight or ten young men sat on the couches out in the clinic waiting room, watching TV. One of them was a smiley-looking chap with dreadlocks who came over to introduce himself. He was not one of the clients, but a worker. He motioned me to follow him outside where, after a gentle handshake I was becoming accustomed to among these fellows, limp and unaggressive, like a tentative gift, he shyly began to tell his story. Ten years earlier, when he was fifteen, Alex—or "Rasta-man," as he had come to be called because of the dreadlocks—had drifted from a village in the countryside into Kisumu where his lack of job and money immediately relegated him to living on the street, essentially homeless. "To survive, I scavenged at the dump, I lived in a handmade shanty," he said. But then he was recruited by the foreign scientists and now his job was to gather in to the project as many as possible of those same street people who still lived hand to mouth. Some were part-time fishermen, some were bicycle taxi drivers. Some got by as had Alex, scavenging at the dump. These were the kinds of young men Bailey and Moses liked to sign up because they saw them as being at higher risk than young men from the more settled elements of society. They would stand to benefit more if the project's hypothesis turned out to be true and, more important for science, because of their casual lifestyle they offered a higher probability of putting the hypothesis to a real test.

Once these young men walked through the door of the clinic, however, they entered a system that was not African by construction but North

American. The clinical trial was an internationally proscribed world with, like a chess game, its own rules. And these rules were stringent. If they were not followed, the results of entire years of work could be termed suspect or thrown out altogether. The list of things around which there was little compromise was a long one and it seemed to trouble Alex greatly. On every fine North American point, Alex's Kenyan view, and especially his view as a person from the street, diverged. He considered that many of the foreign rules and protocols were absurd. For example, the clients were promised health care for two years and received 300 shillings each time they visited the clinic. For the North Americans running and monitoring and ultimately judging the project, it was important that such an exchange never appear to be persuasive or influential. Participants in the trial had to come to it out of their own free will, uninfluenced by extraneous considerations. But for Rasta-man, the poverty of the participants was immensely relevant to their decision to join the study. "The offer of free health care is truly significant," he pronounced, "because otherwise they cannot afford medicine. Perhaps it is the decisive motivation." As well, the 300 shillings was significant because, if you were a *boda-boda* driver, you would have to pedal your bicycle all the way across town with a fare loaded behind you to get only 10% of that. Although it was clear he found the views of the North Americans puzzling, even nonsensical, he confirmed part of the information delivered already by Pabari and Onyango: young men were impatient to get circumcised. They were actively seeking out the clinic to obtain an operation that many could not otherwise afford. A circumcision at a commercial clinic would cost thirty to sixty dollars, or a hundred fares for a *boda-boda* driver.

16

SCIENTIFIC LIFE

*O*N THURSDAY EVENING I HEADED OFF with Maclean, Bailey, and
a young woman named Carolyn Williams, who worked for the
National Institutes of Health in Washington, to one of the Indian restaurants in town in pursuit of their highly rated buffet supper. Williams had
come in earlier that afternoon. She was an ally of UNIM and deeply invested
in the project, having been involved from the moment of its first proposal.
On behalf of the Washington funders, she functioned like a kind of riverboat pilot to steer the researchers through the regulatory and financial
shoals. We entered the restaurant under a large awning, then headed for the
dining area. "Oh no," exclaimed Bailey, "the CDC are here." The Centers for
Disease Control group, about ten of them, who'd also come into town a few
days earlier, occupied a large table in the middle of the room. When they
spotted our foursome, they waved merrily. We acknowledged them self-
consciously, then seated ourselves at a table three away from theirs. While
waiting for our drinks and getting into the mood for the buffet, which had
an appetizing variety of curries and Indian dishes, Ian launched into a story
about a case of chancroid he'd recently come across. The story, delivered in

one of those 'can you believe how bad things are for some people' tones that causes you to shake your head in a mix of wonder and dark amusement, was grim enough that I began to worry about my appetite. I was right about something I'd been long thinking: even dinner couldn't stop microbiologists from talking shop. When Ian finished his story, Carolyn jumped in with one of her own about genital warts. The cycle was broken only when Bailey switched the topic to an entertaining anecdote about how, two decades earlier, he'd had to escort Lauren Hutton, the supermodel and actress, on a visit to the pygmies of the Congo.

In the car on our way to the restaurant, the discussion had been about files. The National Institutes of Health, in an effort to achieve uniformity, had specified a certain type of three-ring binders they wanted UNIM to use, and 2700 of these would have to be purchased. But they were proving hard to come by. "We went to the best stationery store in Kisumu," said Bailey (which happened also to be the only stationery store), "and they didn't have anything like that."

"Order them from Canada," suggested Ian.

"They'd be the wrong size," Bailey said.

"How about from England?" offered Carolyn.

The episode underscored how, in a place like Kisumu, tiny details could be a frustration. "You're always stopped," said Bailey, "by things that in North America you'd take for granted."

Frustrations carrying out research in Africa weren't unique to the AIDS scientists. Earlier that afternoon, when I'd returned to the Nyanza Club, two workmen wearing rubber boots and with spray cans strapped to their backs were emerging from my room. Hurrying to my door, I encountered a fine mist settling upon everything and a smell that was acrid and harsh. Everything was wet: curtains, mosquito netting over the bed, the floor in the bathroom. "What's going on?" I asked Gladys, one of the maids who was hovering, alarmed by my agitation, just outside the door. "They have had to fumigate," she said, "for insects." They'd been exceedingly thorough, my luggage was wet as were the insides of the pair of shoes I'd left on the rack beside the door. I grew even more angry. "What insecticide did they use?" I demanded. Gladys didn't know and the spray boy didn't speak

English. I looked at the package of biscuits on my dresser and the sacks of peanuts I knew I would now have to throw away. Then I had another thought. "Have you sprayed just my room or every room?" I asked. "All of them," said Gladys. Upstairs too? "Yes, all the rooms. We had to do it when everybody was out. Only you have come back." I thought of the Michigan State entomologists and the mosquito movie they were making on their balcony. The Nyanza Club insect spray project wasn't going to leave them very happy.

Our dinner of curried food was delicious, lamb, chicken, numerous vegetarian options, and lots of beer, which we were able to enjoy immensely, especially as it was all flavoured by the fresh breeze blowing in off the lake just to our backs. There were no more stories about diseases or dastardly infections. Halfway into dinner, though, Bailey's cell phone rang. It was Steve Moses calling from Heathrow airport's departure lounge. By next day, he announced, he would be in Kisumu: eight hours to Nairobi overnight, and then the morning flight across the country on Kenya Airways.

Also scheduled to come in was Alan Ronald, a kind of guru for Canadian microbiologists and a great champion of Africa. Dr Ronald had retired some years previously from positions at one of the major hospitals in Winnipeg and the University of Manitoba medical school, where he had been associate dean for research. But he had not gone off to languish on some golf course. Still relatively young and energetic, he had almost immediately headed to Uganda, where he and his wife, Myrna, now spent most of each year in Kampala. There, he agitated to get Western pharmaceutical companies to provide AIDS relief drugs. In his days with the university almost two decades earlier, Ronald had been hugely instrumental in getting the Canadian programs started in Nairobi, Kenya's capital. Now UNIM had asked him to serve as an advisor. When everybody got together, they were going to have a progress meeting.

Thirty-six hours later, on Saturday morning, Moses, Bailey, Ronald, Ian Maclean, and Carolyn Williams gathered at breakfast to discuss their problems. For me, the non-scientist visitor, it was a revealing meeting in that it soon became apparent just how many things there were to worry about, how many things needed attention, and how many things could conceivably go wrong in managing such a project as this. Bailey and Moses, who informally chaired the meeting, reiterated a persistent concern that they were somehow not yet getting a clientele fully typical of young Luo men. Bailey had been worried for some time that the HIV rate among those applying to be clients was too low. At about 10%, it was even lower than the Kisumu average. If they were to have any hope of showing that circumcision was a protection, they would have to work with clients who were at high risk otherwise of contracting the virus. But where would they find them? To get a more at-risk group of people, they asked, should they be sending their recruiters into even rougher parts of town? Williams countered by reiterating the National Institutes of Health's concerns about authenticity and credibility. She didn't want the slightest whiff of coercion or enticement to creep into the study. She pointed out that she'd be quite happy if a certain percentage of potential clients dropped away, since that would be evidence for her bosses back in Washington that the project had standards.

Steve Moses was troubled by something he called the "catch-22" of such a project. What, he asked rhetorically, if, by simply being in the project, the behavior of the participants were to change? "My concern is that the incidence of HIV in the people in the trial won't be as high as in the general population," he said. "And the reason for that will be that people may change their behaviour because of the counselling. They may start doing what we're advising them to do, like wearing condoms. We've seen that in other trials."

His point underlined a true dilemma. In that it would save lives, that would be a good thing, but the downside would be that such a response would render the scientific study useless. The researchers would not get the information they needed or could trust in order to come to definitive conclusions. For that to happen, everybody would have to behave exactly as they would have otherwise or before, but how was that likely to be the case when they were surrounded in their visits to the clinic by posters warning of AIDS and offering safe sex advice? The catch-22 was that the clinic could neither morally nor ethically refrain from offering advice on safe sex and good health.

Alan Ronald brought up another matter, that of post-surgery problems, what the incidences were and how they were handling them. Under the rubric of adverse effects, "AEs" in scientific jargon, the researchers were preoccupied with the need to find out and detail anything unhappy that followed the surgeries. "A 3% rate of some kind of infection is normal," Ronald pointed out. "But a big disaster would be if somebody should die."

Adverse effects were a matter Bailey monitored closely. On the whole, he was satisfied. "Nobody has died," he said. "Nobody's penis fell off." Two percent was their targeted upper limit for incidents of adverse effects. Thus far, 2.5% had been the reality, though most had not been of a severe nature. The worst cases were things like stitches opening up before complete healing had taken place. One fellow, Bailey reported, had sex two times within eight days of his surgery, something he had been adamantly counselled against. Another rode his bicycle home after surgery, and bad hygiene had been a source of further complications, but nothing, he reported, seemed beyond manageable. Then there was more minutiae, such as the tensile strength of the sutures. "Let's face it," Ronald said, "if you're an eighteen- to twenty-year-old guy, you're going to have an erection every day, even the day after surgery."

Bailey then brought up an irritating bugbear: Internal Review Boards. More visitors, also from Washington, were about to descend on them and the potential disruption lurked as a nightmare for the clinic and its staff. The visitors, called "monitors," were coming to sift through all their paperwork. Under newly instituted regulations based on the system employed by drug trials back in North America, monitor teams were to visit each of the projects under National Institutes of Health jurisdiction twice a year. All documents had to be made available so that the monitors could take a fine-tooth comb to them. The concerns prompting the program, Bailey agreed, were legitimate, but he considered it both a layer of irritating extra work, and, perhaps, of questionable effect. Did the system, he asked, really increase protection of the subjects? "The monitors will only look at documents," he said, "they won't interview the staff or the clients. The fact that you have a piece of paper, what does that mean?"

17

THE UNCERTAIN BUSINESS
OF DOING GOOD

A FEW MONTHS AFTER THE VISIT of the monitors, Bob Bailey's worries about what might happen when he opened his project's doors came to fruition. Delving through UNIM's files, the visitors unearthed an irregularity: a piece of paper that was part of the protocol between the researchers and their subjects, and which had to be put on record with all the various partnering institutions, either had not been filed in the offices of the University of Nairobi, or had been lost there. The matter, according to regulations, fell under the category "breach of ethics" and prompted the monitors to pronounce that until things got sorted out, UNIM would be obliged to close its doors. The scientists were dismayed, mostly because they knew that a bureaucratic circus would ensue, a lengthy rigamarole of documents and explanations sent endlessly on the rounds from Nairobi to Winnipeg to Washington to Chicago, institution to institution to institution, desk to desk to desk. Bailey's fear had become his nightmare. "I didn't sleep for nine months," he told me.

Considering the incident in hindsight, one might come to one of two conclusions, each valid within the parameters of its sphere of reference.

On the one hand, it was proper that procedures be strictly followed and a price be exacted for transgressions. On the other, "breach of ethics" seemed a touch dramatic. Was what had happened in that incident really a serious breach of scientific procedure that placed both research and perhaps even human clients at risk, or was it simply another frustration of doing business in Africa? In the end it was all sorted through, but what had it signalled? A salient factor could well have been that the institution flagging the difficulty was the University of Nairobi, of the three UNIM partners, the one that was Africa-based. The entire incident might well have sprung out of issues of relationship, the tenuousness and tensions between hosts and visitors. While Nairobi University was certainly, on paper, an equal partner, it did not furnish the front-line expert researchers; these were the foreigners. Was this incident, then, an occasion for the locals to try to make a point?

It should surprise no one that conflicts might arise in the gigantic laboratory of sub-Saharan Africa. The vast scope of the activity, the deluge of projects, the numbers of foreign-based and foreign-funded undertakings, as well as the power and presumption behind the foreign presence, were a great deal for local communities, including the local scientific community, to accommodate. To accuse all outsiders of arrogance would be unfair to a great many people, but to assess, on the other hand, that they operated with 'presumptions' is not unfair. Scientists of all sorts had headed and were heading into Africa as if to a gold rush town, armed with arguments of being part of an enterprise to save the world. All manner of players could get in on the action, whether their objectives were to make a career, fulfill an altruistic or humanitarian motivation, or simply have an adventure. The foreigners were well-heeled, and entered and left with ease. They possessed sweeping mandates and defined their obligations to the locals largely on their own terms. True, the scientific capabilities of African researchers and African universities were enjoying spinoff benefits, making visible advances under the tutelage of the outsiders, and, yes, critical African problems and crises were being targeted. But the stress and strain couldn't help but be enormous. How much gratitude could Africans be expected to have?

Had the global scientific community not mounted concerted activity, especially around matters like HIV/AIDS, it would have seemed irresponsible and inhumane. But the amount of such activity and the way it was undertaken brought forth a host of questions. These questions must be posed to both African and outsider, and it will take a long time before they are settled in any final way. The emergency aspect of the AIDS crisis distracted from issues that might otherwise naturally accompany so much research and such high levels of external intervention. For instance, some people properly asked about the standard of care that was considered a matter of medical ethics in developed countries on the other side of the world. Was that provided in all African instances? Clinical trials and drug trials have strict protocols; were these always followed in African projects or, in light of the prevailing atmosphere of emergency, were shortcuts taken?

Each time any question was asked, an equal and countervailing point, like the return of a tennis ball, would come in from the other side. Perhaps, some said, it was all right if shortcuts were taken. Someone's imminent death is a compelling argument for making a radical treatment that might otherwise be considered reckless or transgress the niceties of protocol. In this respect, when human trials for an AIDS vaccine loomed on the horizon, arguments were made—frequently by Africans—to fast-track those. Under normal circumstances, such trials had built-in conventions that could stretch them out over a period of years. Could not those be bypassed? The discussions, however, were perpetually complicated. Nothing, upon examination, seemed easy; no argument was clear-cut and able to be cleanly made. The globally accepted protocols had been developed in North America and Europe. To insist they be followed to the letter in African situations meant that Africa and Africans were being treated as equals, not as second-class citizens. Some people believed, however, that the same arguments meant the triumph of abstract global norms over Africa's specific needs. Just because something was right for North America didn't necessarily mean it was right for Africa. What about made-in-Africa compromises? When hundreds of people became infected each day and hundreds more died, it was difficult not to concede this point. Closing down UNIM over the missing paper and calling it an ethics violation was possibly an example of the difficult conundrum-like nature of the questions to be faced.

Strategies themselves in the medical battles came under intense scrutiny. Almost a decade after they had become the treatment of choice in the wealthier parts of North America and Europe, anti-retroviral (ARV) drugs were barely available in Africa. Thousands of people, in Africa and in North America and Europe, were incensed by this. Accusations flew about everything from double standards to pharmaceutical profits being placed ahead of Third World lives. But such a debate could not be held without acknowledging the substantial proviso on the other side of this discussion: helping the millions of African AIDS sufferers by giving them ARVs wasn't simply a matter of paying for the relatively expensive drugs. The real rub was that such treatments were complicated. They would have to be prescribed, delivered, and administered in places where the care system barely existed and, where it did exist, was stretched to the breaking point.

Then there were questions about the relationship between visiting researchers and their hosts. Despite the liberal usage of the term "partners," what levels of participation and control did people in the African countries truly have, whether they be officials or scientists or recipients? Were the research enterprises (including UNIM) really partnerships of even close to equals?

It seemed that science itself had become a problem or at least a culprit. At the 2006 International AIDS Meeting, the biennial gathering of everybody and everything having to do with the world pandemic of AIDS, held in Toronto, South Africa's health minister, Manto Tshabalala-Msimang, set up a public health display that focused neither on anti-retroviral drugs nor on preventions like condom distribution, but on 'natural' potions created out of beetroot, olive oil, garlic, lemons, and African potatoes. The suggestion was that AIDS could be combated by ingesting these potions. To say this "caused a stir" is too kind; the main response from the hundreds of other officials, scientists, and activists, including Bill Clinton and Bill Gates, was outrage. Yet the collision had not come out of the blue. At the very highest levels of the Ministry of Health and the office of the Director General of Health, offices with reach directly into the circle of President Mbeki himself, South Africa had, for some time, not only disdained but publicly attacked the prevailing scientific consensus on the cause and treatment of HIV/AIDS. The disease was caused not by a virus but by poverty, they suggested, and the West's response to the African AIDS crisis was a form of scientific imperialism.

This set the scene for a tempestuous fight where the strategies of the Western AIDS-fighting organizations were thrown into chaos—officials like Mrs Tshabalala-Msimang decried ARVs as "toxic," "damaging," and "poisonous."[1] But what was really going on appeared to be something much bigger, an attack on science itself, or at least an opting out of science. The creation of science or, as it was earlier and more broadly called, "natural history," Mary Louise Pratt declared in *Imperial Eyes,* "asserted an urban, lettered, male authority over the whole of the planet."[2] Was South Africa employing the only means the non-urban, non-male, non-lettered, and, one might add, non-Western had available in order to fight back? It was a ludicrously difficult fight, to be sure, for in any argument against science the very language of discourse is owned by the other side. What's more, given the power of the orthodoxy science has come to possess, one could only suffer ridicule and become marginalized by going up against it. Yet, the fact it was happening deserved examination more serious than simple disdain. What got labelled AIDS denial was in reality a kind of supreme anti-Western gesture couched in the guise of anti-science.

Like many other kinds of outsider projects, scientific research looking into health and disease is bound to bump up naturally against local cultures. The values and traditions of our cultures not only govern what we believe, but prescribe how we behave both as individuals and as communities. They inform us about who we are and where we have come from. They instruct us how to treat our elders as well as our children, the dead as well as the living, our friends as well as strangers. They lay down obligations within our families and toward our neighbours and tell us how to behave toward members of the opposite sex. African societies possess long-standing cultural traditions. Yet, under the stress of their problems, not least the AIDS epidemic, those cultural values have come under pressure. All societies experience change, but what we desire is to have that guided by the values of our culture and not descend on us like some alien comet from outer space. In response not only to the AIDS crisis but to the values and pressures (and power) of the outsider interventionists, can African traditions and values survive? Should they? The Luo in western Kenya have no tradition of circumcision, yet might develop one financed by the US National Institutes of Health and the Canadian Institutes of Health Research. The question has to be, how much are changes in African societies guided by their own cultures and how much are they dictated by money, decisions, and values brought in from afar? Fast on the heels of the pure scientists, the microbiologists and epidemiologists who were first to arrive into the African HIV laboratory, came initiatives propelling behaviour modification. The effects of these, for better or worse, could have an impact on not just a disease, but the shape and values of entire communities for many years into the future. In a highly stressed African society, the outsiders have inordinate power, their word is listened to, their values and priorities have the momentum to swamp the locals, who, knowing what's good for them, learn how to play the game.

This was brought home in stark fashion one night in Nairobi when I went to dinner with a group of foreign researchers and aid workers. Among them was a USAID official whose job placed him in charge of allocating $140 million PEPFAR dollars (George W. Bush's President's Emergency Program for AIDS Relief) in Kenya. That, I observed to him, must make you somewhat highly sought after. "Oh yes," he said, "you have no idea." He had a great deal of experience both in Africa and in the field of HIV/AIDS. But what he was preoccupied with had to do with a curve thrown by values and political realities that came from far outside Africa. The Bush administration had indeed promised a great deal of money, some fifteen billion dollars for all of southern Africa over a number of years. But the reputation of the Bush administration's preferences and tastes had preceded the arrival of its money. As my new acquaintance from USAID acknowledged with some discomfort, an overwhelming number of the proposals coming across his desk, asking for support, were from groups declaring that they wanted money to promote sexual abstinence. The applicants for these grants thought they knew what would get a positive nod from the money donors.

In July 2005, a front-page story in the *Wall Street Journal* reported that an African circumcision trial had been halted. Bob Bailey and Steve Moses were not the only scientists pursuing the question of male circumcision and its possible impact on HIV. In South Africa, a similar study had been underway that was conducted by a French researcher from the Université de Paris. Dr Bertrand Auvert, with his South African colleague, Dr Dirk Taljaard, had enrolled 3000 young men ages eighteen to twenty-four in order to circumcise half of them and, like Bailey and Moses, keep track of the results. In March 2005, nine months before their study was scheduled to come to its end, the Data Safety Monitoring Board (DSMB), the international body to which all scientists undertaking studies must report, ordered Auvert and Taljaard to stop their work. A preliminary unlocking of their data showed the discrepancy in HIV infections between their two cohorts to be an astonishing 65%. In other words, male circumcision, at least in their group, was cutting HIV infection by upwards of two thirds. "It would not be moral," declared the DSMB, "in the light of such astounding data, to continue with a group from whom you were withholding the possibility of becoming circumcised." The study, it would seem, had proved its point; instead of waiting out their term, these young men should be free to get circumcised immediately if they so wished.

Bailey and Moses, naturally, were anxious to know what this development would mean for them and their study. They were not so far along as the South Africans had been, yet might not their data safety monitoring board follow suit and agree that continued trial was not only a waste of time but immoral towards their control group? However, they were quickly reassured that would not be the case. The DSMB that had looked at the end of June at their up-to-the-minute results recommended the Kisumu trial continue. "Obviously," Moses told me after, "they must have felt that there was not a strong enough difference in HIV rates between circumcised and uncircumcised men to stop the trial. This may be because we have not yet had enough follow-up to be able to conclude that there is a real statistical difference, or there may not be one. We don't know."

What the decision to continue also meant was a recognition that a clinical trial should go all the way through to its conclusion. If mass circumcision of African men was going to become a strategy in the battle against AIDS, that decision should not be based on a hypothesis and trials that pointed in the right direction but then were aborted. How scientific was that? There should be at least one and perhaps more than one completed trial in order for anything near scientific certainty.

What Bailey and Moses did know was that about forty of their subjects had become infected with HIV. But since they were still blinded (though their data safety monitoring board was not), they did not know which of their cohorts these men were in, or, if they were from both cohorts, what the balance was. For his part, Bailey found the forty sero-conversions encouraging in that it was a number that was right in the ballpark of their expectations. "We predicted a sero-conversion of about 1% among the circumcised men and 2.5% among the non-circumcised group," he said. "Since forty turns out to be 1.7%, or halfway between our two numbers, we can assume that we are right where we thought we would be." What these numbers also did was reassure them that the issue of behaviour change they had worried about was at least not yet affecting their numbers.

However, they decided to undertake another study to look at the potential impact of behaviour change. They enlisted one of Bailey's graduate students from the University of Illinois to engineer what they called a "disinhibition" study. She was to obtain hard data about the actual behaviour of young men and construct that against the information gathered from the trial's follow-up. They installed two young Kenyans, Evans Otieno and Nicholas Okul, in a house across the road from the clinic, with instructions to interview as many of the young men coming and going from the clinic as possible and try to get answers to the sticky question of whether either participation in the project or a circumcision had altered how they behaved sexually.

Whereas Steve Moses worried about too many of them behaving more carefully, there was also a concern that they behaved less carefully under the illusion that seemed to persist on the street that being circumcised provided "full" protection against HIV. In their interviews, Otieno and Okul were to try to determine how many of them realized this was not the case. It turned out, less than 100%. When I paid a visit they were still some distance from completing their study, but Nicholas Okul confided that, given the volume of information and advice available to the young men concerning HIV and the importance of safe sex practices, depressingly little seemed to have sunk in. Young men had been seated in rooms surrounded by posters proclaiming the dangers of AIDS and given information about condoms. They had been instructed carefully that the jury was still out on the protective capacity of a circumcision and how, even at best, it would be but a partial protection. Yet, in spite of it all, a good number of these young men confessed to Okul and Otieno that the sex they were now having was casual and undertaken with no more care than ever. Nicholas slipped into religious analogy and referred to the recalcitrants as "backsliders." "Talking about AIDS is like preaching the gospel," he sighed, using more church jargon. "You may preach every day, but how many are saved?"

In June of 2006, the UNIM project's clinical trial landed again in front of the Data Safety Monitoring Board. Again, Bailey and Moses waited on pins and needles for the DSMB decision. Again, their project was spared, but only provisionally. They were told they would be looked at once more in another six months. When that happened, on December 12, 2006, at least a year in advance of their scheduled completion, their research project was at last halted. As the monitors had pronounced eighteen months earlier with the South African research, their numbers were so good that it would be unethical to the young men in the control group to hold them back any longer from being circumcised if they so wanted. Without completing a full clinical trial, those championing circumcision had, by a 2–1 margin, proved their point. With additional authors Kawango Agot, Carolyn Williams, Ian Maclean, Dr J.O. Ndinya-Achola, and a couple of others, Bailey and Moses published the results of their study, such as it was and as far as it had gone, in the British medical journal, The Lancet. Looking at 2784 young men in Luoland, they reported, the two-year incidence of HIV among the half of them who were circumcised was 2.1%; among the control group, the half who had not been circumcised, 4.2%. "The reduction in the risk of acquiring HIV was 53%." It was one of the few bits of good news on the HIV front that year.

18

LEAVING AFRICA

I LEFT KISUMU ON A SPECTACULAR late October morning. The sun shimmered off the brilliant emerald-green foliage, Lake Victoria sparkled like a necklace of diamonds. The Kenya Airways flight to Nairobi departed at 9:00 a.m. There was another flight on a rival airline, East Africa Airways, scheduled for 6:00 in the evening, that would have got me to Nairobi in lots of time for the 10:00 p.m. British Airways flight to London and then Toronto, but two separate ticket agents urged me to go for the earlier flight, even though it meant sitting in Nairobi all day. "East Africa has been flirting with bankruptcy," I was told, "there is no saying which will be their last trip, maybe the one just before the one you need." I placed my bag on the conveyer belt and watched two hefty Kenyan politicians and two Indian businessmen, the politicians in three-piece suits and the businessmen in golf shirts and slacks, proceed out to the small jet ahead of me. Though many people in Kenya are desperately poor, I was reminded once more that not everybody is: the fingers and wrists of all four men were weighted down with clunky gold watches and bracelets and rings.

Once in the air, I settled back and absorbed the hum of the engines. The lone attendant brought coffee in a plastic cup. I pressed my forehead to the window and looked down. Seeing the world from the height of an airplane is something I have always liked. This was a small plane and we didn't have enough altitude for a truly dramatic overview, but there was enough peace and perspective that into my mind came a roil of thoughts. I thought about the past dozen years of my own trips. Down there somewhere, though a long way in the other direction, was Angola. What had become of it? The most recent opinion had it as an economic player, especially in natural resources now because of oil, though most of that was under the thumb of ironclad contracts with the Chinese. But Angola had also been named one of the top ten most corrupt countries in the world with roughly six billion dollars every year simply vanishing while 70% of the population got by on less than a half dollar a day. Closer, somewhere, in fact, just over my right shoulder, lay Rwanda; deceivingly green and verdant should you be flying over it, but still, one had to believe, a boil needing to be lanced periodically. A handful of people had been punished for last decade's atrocities, but everyone wondered when things would next erupt. The Tutsis were now in undisputed control while the Hutus stewed. Nairobi, of course, lay straight ahead, its shantytown sex worker clinic still operating, but the clues everyone wanted in order to complete the puzzle remaining elusive. And, of course, way far to the south, Zimbabwe had become, with every passing day, a more worrisome chaos for both its own people and for the world.

Providing at least a small bit of perspective, of course, were those things that were timeless. How many cubic metres of water had tumbled over Victoria Falls's cataracts in those dozen years since I had been there? And Livingstone, was he still looking out over it through the bronze eyes of his statue?

The people I had followed, filmed, and written about had scattered. Some were still in Africa, others long since returned to Europe and North America to continue their work or write their papers. I had managed to remain in touch with a few. But as time moved on, what sense did they have that they had accomplished what they had set out to do? What did their work mean, in light especially of the passing of time? What did *my* work mean?

The narrative of Africa continued to throw up unsettling contradictions. A particularly troubling one, newly placed on the table, concerned emigration statistics for African university graduates, which told us that a 'brain drain' was happening. Some analysts declared that as many as 50,000 PhDs, or 30% of the continent's university-educated professionals, were now living and working far from home, in Britain, Europe, and North America. Others put the number even higher: 70,000. Just when their home countries needed them most, Africa's best and brightest were leaving and doing so in huge and deeply troubling numbers. The British government's Commission for Africa dramatized the issue by suggesting that the number of skilled migrants leaving the continent was almost identical to the number of foreign technical experts being sent in as part of Western NGO projects or foreign aid packages. In other words, for every expert sent to help Africa—a medical professional, engineer, lawyer, governmental analyst, teacher, environmental planner, agricultural researcher—an educated African national was exiting in the other direction. An economist at Leeds Metropolitan University, Professor Alex Nunn, undertook a study of the migration for the British Association of University Teachers (AUT) and allowed that while migration statistics are notoriously imprecise, the trend was incontestable—as was its price tag. "A larger home-grown skills base would be beneficial for all sorts of reasons," he said in an e-mail to me, "including lowering dependency on foreign expertise which, as history tells us, does not come value free." Then there were the social costs that would plague the continent well into the future, the lost social knowledge, history, local ways of thinking, and an overreliance on externally developed knowledge.

Commenting on people's migration is a delicate business, of course, because nobody in a globalized world is going to begrudge anyone's right to pursue better opportunities for security or happiness for themselves or their family. But in light of the matter of relationships and interconnections, this was a disturbing story. If one lamented what was going on (as one should), one also had to face up to the hypocrisy of that lament. The irony was that Western countries were benefiting greatly from the skills and education the migration of educated Africans brought with them, so were not at all idle or passive observers. The Commission for Africa, for example, accused the British health care system of actively poaching African professionals, and levelled the same charge at Canada. One industry observer commented that if it weren't for Zimbabweans and Zambians, the British health care system would collapse. Nurses in those countries are trained by a system held over from colonial days that gives them more all-around skills than graduates of current Western programs, so they are considered very valuable to any program in which they settle. Canada not only benefited from the skills brought by foreign-trained doctors and nurses, a number of provinces had undertaken deliberate ventures to recruit them.

This was a kind of foreign aid in reverse, happening, to Africa's great misfortune, just at the time when traditional foreign aid was coming under increased and severe scrutiny. Authors like former World Bank economist and professor at New York University William Easterly were turning out books with titles like *The White Man's Burden: Why the West's Efforts to Aid the Rest Have Done So Much Ill and So Little Good*. Published in 2006, Easterly's book charged that despite half a trillion dollars of foreign aid to Africa over the past forty years, poverty in many countries there had only worsened. Robert Calderisi, another one-time World Bank economist, followed with his book, *The Trouble with Africa; Why Foreign Aid Isn't Working*, in which he laid the blame at the feet of corrupt local leadership and a global economy that had left Africa behind. The immediate and simple message: why bother? All initiatives were surely, in the end, too troublesome—good money after bad into situations we outsiders apparently neither understood nor could control.

It should have been heartening how, in my country, Canada, two champions of Africa were among the most consistently admired figures on the public stage. The UN special envoy for AIDS, Stephen Lewis, and the former peacekeeping commander from Rwanda, General Roméo Dallaire, were passionate presenters who could always draw crowds. Yet, it would have been seen as impolitic if not impolite to point out that their narratives were not about successes, but about failures. The Africa they were so passionate about was a place where genocides went on that the rest of the world could not figure out how to stop, and virus-fed epidemics devastated whole countries, and where useful intervention was beyond everybody's reach. What would it take, one had to wonder, in order to make the great leap across such perplexities and land in the territory of true sisterhood and brotherhood?

In the airplane, a funny little song I'd first learned in Sunday school, well before it was appropriated by Disney, improbably (though perhaps not so) jumped into my head. "It's a small world after all, it's a small, small, world . . . ," an almost silly ditty I couldn't get out of my head. Global economies and air transportation tell us the world is small, yet, it's not a small world at all. I knew just by looking out the airplane window that it was a very big world; the trips across even just one country like Kenya, and certainly in and out of it, could seem endless. And Africa in total was huge. I'd once seen a map that showed that within the outline of the continent of Africa could be held all of Europe east of the Urals, plus Scandinavia, China, India, the continental United States, Argentina, and the islands of New Zealand. We weren't so high that I couldn't make out what was down below. The vast expanse of landscape appeared empty, but it was not empty, for hidden in the forests and the curls of hills and shadows of plateaus were villages and people and farms and shops and animals. Thousands of them.

In Nairobi, instead of going into the city and trying to cope with that, I had decided I would spend the day at Kenyatta National Airport. There was reading to do, I could indulge in people watching. I located a place away from the main check-in area and passed a couple of hours just observing the comings and goings. I left the terminal and went for a walk; the day had turned hot with a dusty breeze. I got a sandwich from a kiosk. Eventually, I went through passport control and entered the departure zone. The concourse up there, as in any big airport, was lined with shops selling souvenirs to tourists and visitors: T-shirts with African scenes, giraffes and zebras and rhinos. Colourful bolts of printed cloth. Coffee-table sculptures of elephants carved from ebony. Masai spears—though I wasn't sure how those would fare as carry-on luggage. The shops also sold bottles of duty-free liquor from Britain and jars of perfume from France. At the end of the concourse, a coffee lounge had CNN on its television. The World Series was on and highlights from a baseball game played several hours earlier (in America it was now the middle of the night) were being shown.

I returned to the corridor where immediately I became entangled among a throng of forty or fifty children herded by some adults with clipboards who managed to look both official and caring at the same time. We all soon ended up in the same waiting area off the main corridor. The children, who ranged from mere babes in arms to perhaps ten or twelve years old, were all dressed in identical blue T-shirts with tags around their necks. They scrambled up onto the seats and tried to sit still. A couple cried, a few nodded off to sleep. I tried to surmise who they were and where they might be going. Their handlers all spoke in French. Finally I got an explanation from one of the women minding them. "Orphans from Darfur," she said, the latest wartorn hellhole in nearby Sudan, on their way to Belgium. It was a huge world. But also a very small one.

NOTES

INTRODUCTION

1. Quoted by Joanna Bourke in a review of *Inventing Human Rights, Harper's* magazine (May 2007): 90.

2. Tim Jeal, *Dr Livingstone* (London: Heinemann, 1973), 2.

3. Ibid.

4. Mary Louise Pratt, *Imperial Eyes, Travel Writing and Transculturation* (New York: Routledge, 1992), 8.

5. William Easterly, *The White Man's Burden, Why the West's Efforts to Aid the Rest Have Done So Much Ill and So Little Good* (New York: Penguin Group, 2006).

6. Robert Calderisi, *The Trouble with Africa: Why Foreign Aid Isn't Working* (London: Palgrave Macmillan, 2007).

CHAPTER 1

1. There are many accounts of this, an excellent one being Ryszard Kapuscinski, who, in 1975, had called it a "mad senseless war in which nobody knew anything, the opponents couldn't tell each other apart until the last second, and you could be blown away without fighting simply because of the crazy screw-ups." See *Another Day of Life* (New York: Harcourt Brace Jovanovich, 1987), 48.

CHAPTER 2

1. MPLA, Movimento Popular para a Libertacao de Angola; FNLA, Frente Nacional da Libertacao de Angola; Unita, União Nacional para a Independência Total de Angola. By the 1990s MPLA and Unita remained the rivals.

CHAPTER 3

1. David Sogge, *Sustainable Peace, Angola's Recovery* (Harare: SARDC, 1992), 19.

CHAPTER 4

1. Rotimi Sankore, quoted here from the article, "Behind the Image: Poverty and 'Development Pornography'" (<www.Pambazuka.org>, 2005), is a journalist and rights campaigner who has written widely on history, politics, and culture in Africa.

2. Cited in Mary Louise Pratt, *Imperial Eyes, Travel Writing and Transculturation* (New York: Routledge, 1992), 70.

CHAPTER 9

1. Philip Gourevitch, *We Wish to Inform You That Tomorrow We Will Be Killed with Our Families, Stories from Rwanda* (New York: Farrar, Straus and Giroux, 1998).

2. A search for ICTR, International Criminal Tribunal for Rwanda, produced by the United Nations, provides a wealth of information about all charges, defendants, trials, participants, and sentences.

CHAPTER 11

1. Urbanization in Africa and the 'informal' nature of that is a field of active and growing study. The following three papers were presented at the symposium, Urbanization in Africa, University of Toronto, February 2004: Mamadou Diouf (University of Michigan), "West African Cities"; Winnie Mitullah (University of Nairobi), "Tapping Opportunities in Decentralized Governance and Informal Activities for Urban Development in East African Countries"; and Richard Stren (University of Toronto), "An Urbanizing Africa: The Challenge of Informality."

CHAPTER 12

1. Neuffer, Minow, and Mutua quoted by Alexander Zahar and Susan Rohol in "The International Tribunal for Rwanda," in *Genocide at the Millennium: A Critical Bibliographic Review,* vol. 5, ed. Samuel Totten (New Brunswick, NJ: Transaction Publishers, 2005), 214.

2. Hugh McCullum, *The Angels Have Left Us, the Rwandan Tragedy and the Churches* (Geneva: WWC Publications, 1998).

3. Roméo Dallaire, *Shake Hands with the Devil* (Toronto: Random House, 2003).

4. Jean Kambanda, prime minister from April 8, 1994, to July 17, 1994, was indicted by the tribunal and pleaded guilty to genocide and crimes against humanity. He is serving life imprisonment.

5. Zahar and Rohol, "International Tribunal," 216. Alexander Zahar served as a senior legal officer to President Judge Mose during the Rwanda Tribunal before moving to the Yugoslav Tribunal in The Hague. He now teaches law in Australia.

6. Ibid.

7. Ibid., 220, 221.

8. In January 2007, Pastor Elizaphan Ntakirutimana, then eighty-three years old, died in a hospital in Arusha, Tanzania.

CHAPTER 17

1. Tshabalala-Msimang's views on ARVs are from an article by Michael Specter, "The Denialists," *The New Yorker* (March 12, 2007): 33.

2. Pratt, *Imperial Eyes*, 38.

SELECTED BIBLIOGRAPHY

BOOKS

Bonner, Raymond. *At the Hand of Man, Peril and Hope for Africa's Wildlife*. New York: Knopf, 1993.

Calderisi, Robert. *The Trouble with Africa; Why Foreign Aid Isn't Working*. London: Palgrave Macmillan, 2007.

Churchill, Winston S. *My African Journey*. London: Holland Press, 1908.

Dallaire, Roméo. *Shake Hands with the Devil*. Toronto: Random House, 2003.

Easterly, William. *The White Man's Burden, Why the West's Efforts to Aid the Rest Have Done So Much Ill and So Little Good*. New York: Penguin Group, 2007.

Gourevitch, Philip. *We Wish to Inform You That Tomorrow We Will Be Killed with Our Families, Stories from Rwanda*. New York: Farrar, Straus and Giroux, 1998.

Hochschild, Adam. *King Leopold's Ghost*. New York: Houghton Mifflin, 1999.

Jeal, Tim. *Dr Livingstone*. London: Heinemann, 1973.

Kapuscinski, Ryszard. *Another Day of Life*. New York: Harcourt Brace Jovanovich, 1987.

_____. *The Soccer War*. London: Granta Books, 1990.

Lewis, Stephen. *Race Against Time*. Toronto: Anansi, 2005.

Markham, Beryl. *West with the Night*. Boston: Houghton Mifflin, 1942; San Francisco: North Point Press, 1983.

Marshall, George, and David Poling. *Schweitzer, a Biography*. New York: Doubleday, 1971.

Matthiessen, Peter. *African Silences*. New York: Random House, 1991.

_____. *The Tree Where Man Was Born*. New York: Penguin Books, 1995.

McCullum, Hugh. *Africa's Broken Heart*. Geneva: WWC Publications, 2007.

_____. *The Angels Have Left Us, the Rwandan Tragedy and the Churches*. Geneva: WWC Publications, 1998.

Moorhead, Alan. *The White Nile*. London: Hamish Hamilton, 1960.

Nolen, Stephanie. *28 Stories of AIDS in Africa*. Toronto: Random House Canada, 2007.

Power, Samantha. *A Problem from Hell: America and the Age of Genocide*. New York: Basic Books, 2002.

Pratt, Mary Louise. *Imperial Eyes, Travel Writing and Transculturation*. New York: Routledge, 1992.

Rice, Edward. *Captain Sir Richard Francis Burton, a Biography*. New York: Charles Scribner's Sons, 1990.

Sogge, David. *Sustainable Peace, Angola's Recovery*. Harare: SARDC, 1992.

Theroux, Paul. *Dark Star Safari, Overland from Cairo to Capetown*. New York: Houghton Mifflin, 2003.

Waugh, Evelyn. *A Tourist in Africa*. London: Chapman & Hall Ltd, 1960.

Papers and Articles

Bourke, Joanna. "Review of *Inventing Human Rights*." *Harper's* (May 2007).

Diouf, Mamadou. "West African Cities." Paper presented at the symposium, Urbanization in Africa, University of Toronto, February 2004.

Mitullah, Winnie. "Tapping Opportunities in Decentralized Governance and Informal Activities for Urban Development in East African Countries." Paper presented at the symposium, Urbanization in Africa, University of Toronto, February 2004.

Specter, Michael. "The Denialists." *The New Yorker* (March 12, 2007): 33.

Stren, Richard. "An Urbanizing Africa: The Challenge of Informality." Paper presented at the symposium, Urbanization in Africa, University of Toronto, February 2004.

Bailey, Robert, Moses, Stephen, and co-authors Parker, Agot, Maclean, Krieger, Williams, Campbell, and Ndinya-Achola. "Male Circumcision for HIV Prevention in Young Men in Kisumu, Kenya: A Randomised Controlled Trial." *The Lancet* 369 (2007): 643–56.

Zahar, Alexander, and Rohol, Susan. "The International Criminal Tribunal for Rwanda." In *Genocide at the Millennium, A Critical Bibliographic Review*, ed. Samuel Totten. Volume 5. New Brunswick, NJ: Transaction Publishers, 2005.